SECOND EDITION

THE INEFFICIENT STOCK MARKET

What Pays Off and Why

Robert A. Haugen

Emeritus Professor of Finance, University of California, Irvine

Prentice
Hall

UPPER SADDLE RIVER, NEW JERSEY 07458

Library of Congress Cataloging-in-Publication Data

Haugen, Robert A.
    The inefficient stock market : what pays off and why / Robert A. Haugen.—2nd ed.
    p. cm.
    ISBN 0-13-032366-7
    1. Stocks. 2. Stock exchanges. I. Title.

HG4661 H36 2001
332.63'22—dc21   2001021308

Executive Editor: *Mickey Cox*
Managing Editor: *Gladys Soto*
Editor-in-Chief: *P.J. Boardman*
Assistant Editor: *Cheryl Clayton*
Editorial Assistant: *Melanie Olsen*
Media Project Manager: *Bill Minick*
Marketing Manager: *Joshua McClary*
Marketing Assistant: *Christopher Bath*
Production Manager: *Gail Steier de Acevedo*
Production Coordinator: *Kelly Warsak*
Permissions Coordinator: *Suzanne Grappi*
Associate Director, Manufacturing: *Vincent Scelta*
Manufacturing Buyer: *Natacha St. Hill Moore*
Cover Designer: *Bruce Kenselaar*
Composition: *Carlisle Communications*
Full-Service Project Management: *Carlisle Communications*
Printer/Binder: *RRD/Harrisonburg*
Cover Printer: *Phoenix Color Corp.*

10 9 8 7 6 5 4 3 2 1

ISBN 0-13-032366-7

CONTENTS

PREFACE

Factor models have been widely employed in the investments business for decades. Quantitatively oriented managers have used them to control the month-to-month variation in the *differences* between the returns to their stock portfolios and the returns to the stock indices to which they are benchmarked. These models employ a wide variety of ad hoc factors that have been shown to be effective in predicting the *risk* of a stock portfolio.

Factor models have also been widely discussed in academic finance. Finance professors have long searched for the factors that account for the extent to which returns are correlated stock to stock. The professors have correctly concluded that the correlations can be *explained* by a few factors, such as unexpected changes in industrial production, inflation, or interest rates. This is not to say that these few factors can match the success of the wide variety of ad hoc factors used in the business for *forecasting* risk.

The professors have also used factor models to *explain* why stocks have differential expected returns. These models are theoretical in nature, and are derived under the assumption that pricing in the stock market is efficient and rational. If it is not, a wide variety of ad hoc factors may be useful in explaining and *predicting* expected stock returns.

Until recently, ad hoc factor models have not been employed to predict the expected return to stock portfolios. Surprisingly, the factor models are much more powerful in predicting expected return than they are in predicting risk. The purpose of this book is to demonstrate and explain the nature of this power.

I wish to thank Teimur Abasov, David Friese, and David Olson for research assistance. I have also benefited from the comments of Mark Fedenia, Joseph Finnerty, Jeremy Gold, Tiffany Haugen, Thomas Krueger, Robert Marchesi, Cheryl McCaughey, Ray Parker, Neal Stoughton, Manuel Tarrazo, and Ole Jakob Wold. Much of the original work was done jointly with Nardin Baker. The idea for this book was suggested to me by Paul Donnelly.

This book is dedicated to The Mud, thick as they may be.

1

INTRODUCTION

BRAINWASHED

For the past 40 years, a total of approximately one million unsuspecting MBA students have been thoroughly indoctrinated by business schools with the belief that stock markets are efficient.

An efficient market always prices every stock correctly. That is, the price of each stock accurately reflects the very best estimate of all the dividends to be received over the life of the company. Given those projected dividends and the price established by the efficient market, you can expect to earn a return on the stock that is perfectly fair, given the stock's relative risk and the returns that are available elsewhere in the financial markets.

True advocates of efficient markets believe this is the case at *all* times and for *every* stock.

If it *is* true, you can pick stocks by throwing darts. But forget darts! Your best investment is really a simple index fund—a fund that invests in a broad market index like the S&P 500.

Think stocks are too risky? Then lower your risk by putting a sufficient amount of your money in the bank instead of in the index fund. You see, risk management is really easy in an efficient market.

Trying to smooth the earnings of your company through accounting adjustments? You're simply wasting your time! The efficient market sees right through the numbers you report—it *knows* the real numbers, so you might as well report them in the first place.

Delaying making a business investment because you think interest rates are too high? Another mistake! Interest rates are *never* too high. They always reflect the best possible estimate of future inflation as well as a fair level of compensation to bondholders for consuming later so that *you* can invest now.

By the way, it makes no difference whether you finance that investment by selling bonds or stock. The efficient market prices both fairly. In fact, if you raise money by selling any type of financial claim on the profits of your firm, given its best estimate of your firm's future profits and given its sound analysis of the nature of the claim, the efficient market will price it fairly. So go ahead. Issue a few AA debentures—or a lot of junk bonds. Make them convertible, callable, zero coupon, etc. The efficient market will assign any or all a price that is correct and fair. The total value of your firm will be unaffected no matter what you do.[1]

Pretty heady stuff.

If the market is efficient, the world turns into a pretty simple place — at least for the people in academic finance.

However, don't throw away all those investment and business books you've collected over the years.

Because it's *not*.

Efficient, that is.

Although efficient markets people *still* go around saying there is a "mountain" of evidence supporting their hypothesis, the truth of the matter is that it's a very old mountain that's eroding rapidly into the sea.

A new and growing mountain of evidence is completely contradictory to the notion of efficient markets.

And contradictory in a big way. It's now very clear that the market makes BIG mistakes in pricing stocks. It *doesn't* see through reported accounting numbers. It's typically overly optimistic about to-be-reported earnings.[2] It projects that successful firms will continue their success for far too long into the future.[3]

And the list goes on and on.

And what about the one million MBAs who went to business school to *learn* about investing and running a business?

They should ask for their money back.

THE EVOLUTION OF ACADEMIC FINANCE

As a rather ancient ex-academic, I like to distinguish between The Old Finance, Modern Finance, and The New Finance.

Figure 1–1 summarizes their basic features. The top of the figure shows the time frame over which each existed.

See the blocked-off period during the 1960s? This is when I received my formal education in finance. Note that I went to school when Modern Finance was relatively young and when The Old Finance was dying.

An interesting time indeed.

My professors, groomed in The Old Finance, were mostly expert in the fields of accounting and law. In fact, accounting and law are the basic foundations of The Old Finance.

Of all the books I was asked to master, two stand out clearly in my mind.

The first was called *Security Analysis*.[4] It was written by Benjamin Graham and David Dodd, and we used it to study investments. Graham and Dodd spent most of their book showing us the painful process of adjusting accounting statements so that the earnings and assets of different companies could be directly compared.

FIGURE 1–1 The Evolution of Academic Finance

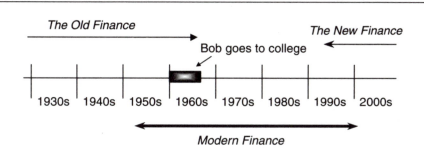

The Old Finance

Theme:	Analysis of Financial Statements and the Nature of Financial Claims
Paradigms:	*Analysis of Financial Statements* (Graham & Dodd) *Uses and Rights of Financial Claims* (Dewing)
Foundation:	Accounting and Law

Modern Finance

Theme:	Valuation Based on Rational Economic Behavior
Paradigms:	*Optimization* (Markowitz) *Irrelevance* (Modigliani & Miller) *CAPM* (Sharpe, Lintner & Mossen) *EMH* (Fama)
Foundation:	Financial Economics

The New Finance

Theme:	Inefficient Markets
Paradigms:	Inductive *ad hoc* Factor Models
	Expected Return (Haugen) *Risk* (Chen, Roll & Ross) *Behavioral Models* (Kahneman & Tversky)
Foundation:	Statistics, Econometrics, and Psychology

This was mostly very *dry* stuff and not too interesting.

But, to their credit, our professors taught us a craft. We learned what to watch out for in accounting statements and how to make the proper adjustments. *Useful* stuff.

The second book was called *The Financial Policy of Corporations*.[5] It was written in two great volumes by Arthur Stone Dewing. *This* book made *Security Analysis* look like a Stephen King thriller. In *Policy,* we learned the legal rights of financial claims—*in great detail.* We learned the laws relating to merger and acquisition as well as those governing bankruptcy and reorganization.

Once again, our professors were teaching us a craft. We were preparing for our future. As possible future financial executives, we needed to know the rules of the game if we had to merge or go bust, as well as the legal impediments on our firm's behavior created by the financial claims that were there today or might be there tomorrow.

Unbeknownst to me at the time, the birth of Modern Finance occurred when, early in the 1950s, a Ph.D. student named Harry Markowitz created a dazzling new tool for building stock portfolios called *portfolio optimization.*

Suppose you have a population of stocks, each having a different expected future return and a different level of risk.[6] You want to construct a portfolio of these stocks that has a 10% expected return. Harry showed how much to invest in each stock so as to have the lowest possible variability in periodic return, given our 10% expected return objective.

Although portfolio optimization would ultimately prove to be of great value to the world, Harry's new tool would lie almost unnoticed for more than a decade.

In the middle of that decade, two economists named Modigliani and Miller introduced the second major paradigm of Modern Finance—*the M&M Irrelevance Theorems.*

What was irrelevant?

Apparently all the rules and laws we had been studying in Dewing's *Policy.* M&M claimed that the nature and composition of the right side of a firm's balance sheet—its financial claims—didn't matter. What did matter was the nature and composition of the left side—its assets and investments. How you packaged, for delivery to the claimants, the fruits of those investments had no impact whatsoever on the total value of the firm.

Although M&M didn't say so at the time, the Irrelevance Theorems assumed an efficient market. Only if all possible claims are fairly priced will their nature have no impact on firm value.[7] If you know that your stock is being priced at half its fair value by an inefficient market, issuing more of it to *new* stockholders will not be in the interests of your *existing* stockholders.

The third and fourth paradigms of Modern Finance appeared at approximately the same time in the early 1960s.

The *Capital Asset Pricing Model* (CAPM) assumed *universal*[8] and *unrestricted*[9] use of Harry Markowitz's optimization tool. If *everyone* built their stock portfolio by optimizing, how would this affect pricing in the securities market?

The answer:

Under these conditions, a *single* factor would make one stock different from another in its expected return. In the world of CAPM, investors hold widely diversified portfolios. In fact, in the simple form of the model, we all invest in the market index. Risk is then variability in return to that index. The risk of an individual stock is measured by its contribution to that variability.

They called this contribution *beta*—the sensitivity of a security's periodic return to changes in the periodic return to the market index.

The ascension of Modern Finance was complete with the introduction of the fourth paradigm. Interestingly, it came from the same campus as Harry's tool.

Again, a Ph.D. student.

Eugene F. Fama dreamed of the *efficient market* and wrote of it in his dissertation.

Not much in the way of rigorous theory here. Just a contention consistent with some initial empirical evidence. Stock prices appeared to change randomly from one period to the next. If stocks were always responding instantly and accurately to the appearance of new and unanticipated information (which must come in randomly if it truly can't be anticipated), prices would move randomly as well.

All in all, this looked like an impressive set of paradigms at the time.

Impressive, but *threatening* to my old professors.

Given these paradigms, what good would come from standardizing accounting statements? The statements had already been "standardized" in the minds of countless investors looking for bargains. These investors had acted. Prices had been set.

To reflect the *true* level of earnings.

Standardizing accounting statements was now seen as a colossal waste of time. Learning how to do it as well.

And the nature of financial claims was also irrelevant.

The craft of finance and the teachings of my old professors had been rendered *obsolete*.

It's not nice to be obsolete.

The professors of The Old Finance fought very hard to retain their relevance. The battles of this intellectual war are still recorded in the pages of ancient issues of the *Journal of Finance* and the *American Economic Review*.

But the professors of The Old lost most of these battles, and eventually they lost the war itself.

New professors came to the university. With very different skills. Many came from economics departments, and they had been trained to theorize under the assumption of *rational economic behavior*.

How would the market behave if emotions or biases never came into play? How would the market behave if everyone thought through the implications of every decision to the finest detail?

With initial empirical support for their paradigms and the *true* triumphs that came with the introduction of models for the pricing of options, Modern Finance took off, seeming to possess the characteristics of a true paradigm shift. It became the dominant discipline in business schools, and it carried great influence in the real world.

Those who would dare to question the validity of the paradigms—especially that of efficient markets—were summarily dismissed as *gauche*.

Those who dared to publish papers contradicting the paradigms were ridiculed. Their studies were supposedly replete with bias. And their methods, of course, were presumed naïve.

Their studies included only firms that survived the study period—survival bias. They used earnings numbers that may not have been publicly available at the time they bought the stocks—look-ahead bias. They probably spun the computer countless times until they got an interesting result—data mining. They didn't take transactions costs into account. They didn't risk-adjust their returns. They didn't test for statistical significance. Their results weren't robust in different time periods.

On and on . . .

However, we *now* know these initial results were *on the mark.*[10]

But summarily *dismissed.*

Fortunately, even when the mud is thick, truth always makes its way to the surface.

Modern Finance received a real punch in the nose in 1976 in the form of a study out of the University of Iowa.[11] Roseff and Kinney discovered that January was a very unusual month for the stock market. The returns to an equally weighted stock index were remarkably high in the first month of the year.

Then the results came pouring in.

Most of the premium return came in the first two weeks,[12] normally to the smaller stocks.[13] The effect was prevalent in most of the stock markets throughout the world.[14] Stocks that paid no dividends were particularly affected,[15] as were stocks that had been poor performers in the past.[16]

Modern Finance now faced a myriad of *anomalies* coming from every direction.

Anomaly: evidence of behavior that contradicts accepted theoretical prediction.

Anomalies: stocks with relatively high current-earnings yields produce relatively high future returns.[17] Stocks with relatively high book-to-price ratios also.[18] Short-term reversals in stock price movements. Intermediate-term momentum and longer-term reversals.[19] Underreaction to financing through sales of stock[20] and to announcements of stock repurchase programs.[21]

And this is but a short list.

Anomalies: statistically significant, risk-adjusted results, net of transaction costs, which can't be explained on the basis of the bias problems discussed above.

But that's okay. After all, they're only *anomalies.* Fair warning. Anyone who takes them seriously can expect to be dismissed as gauche.

But alas! There are *too many* to be dismissed.

And now Modern Finance begins to teeter.

And a New Finance appears.

Discard those theories that obviously have *no* predictive power. Discard the requirement that all explanations must be based on rational economic behavior. Look carefully at the data and measure accurately without preconception. Discard the tradition that you must *first* model without looking and *then* verify. Carefully measure behavior first, and then find *reasonable* and *plausible* explanations for what you see. Ascension of the *ad hoc,* expected return, factor model. The measure of any model's relative merit: the *unmined, out-of-sample, relative accuracy of its predictions.*

Go back to teaching students a *craft* rather than a *religion.*

The drummers sound, the cannons roar, and a second war begins.

The side that *predicts best* must ultimately win this war, for the simple reason that the world places great value on accurate prediction.

Students will want to claim that value.

And business school *deans* will want to satisfy their demands.

The war is long and bitterly fought. Obsolescence is, once again, on the line. The students are coming to the university, once again, to learn the craft of finance.

Unfortunately, many of the "modern" professors haven't learned the craft themselves.

So they must be retooled.

WHY YOU NEED TO READ THIS BOOK

The inefficient market makes many mistakes in pricing stocks. These mistakes result in *tendencies.* Stocks with particular characteristics *tend* to produce premium returns.

The market has a map with topography measured in expected return. There are places to go on that map that are *evil.* If you go there, you will underperform badly in the long run. There are *good* places, too. Go there and you will be rewarded.

In this book, you will learn how to measure the payoffs to stock characteristics (factors). My book *The New Finance: The Case for an Over-reactive Stock Market*[22] is about the positive payoff to cheapness. In this book, we will reconfirm the critical importance of cheapness. However, we will also discuss, among other things, the payoffs to risk, liquidity, profitability, and a stock's performance in past periods.

And, in the tradition of The New Finance, we shall seek reasonable explanations for these payoffs. Some of these explanations *are* consistent with rational behavior. However, the contractual environment in which this behavior takes place is, itself, irrational, creating agency problems that induce the behavior. Some payoffs are rooted in purely irrational human behavior. For these, we look toward the field of psychology.

You will also discover a new kind of stock.

You've probably heard of growth stocks and value stocks. Both reside at different places on the market's map. But there are other places on the map where few have ever gone.

Such as the land of Super Stocks.

A Super Stock portfolio has the following characteristics: The companies in the portfolio are, *on average,* big, liquid, and well-known. They have low risk, and they are financially sound. They are highly profitable in all dimensions. And while they have had strong relative performance over the past year, they are still selling at dirt-cheap prices relative to their cash flow, earnings, and dividends.

This is a dream profile. It is the profile of a portfolio that can be expected to produce the best returns in the future.

No individual stock has the complete profile. If a stock were complete, the inefficient market would price it up until it was expensive rather than cheap.

Nevertheless, it is easy to construct a complete portfolio by assembling incomplete stocks that have components of the complete profile.

Want to learn how to build such a portfolio?

Want to learn what pays off and why?

Keep reading.

Notes

1. Technically, even if the market is efficient, your choice between debt and equity may affect your tax bill because interest payments are deductible while dividend payments are not. Also, the presence of debt may make you, as manager, do things you wouldn't ordinarily do—like try harder to make enough money to meet the interest charges.
2. See P. Dechaow and R. Sloan, "Returns to Contrarian Investment Strategies: Tests of Naïve Expectations Hypotheses," *Journal of Financial Economics,* 43 (1997).
3. See R. La Porta, J. Lakonishok, A. Shleifer, and R. Vishny, "Good News for Value Stocks: Further Evidence on Market Efficiency," *Journal of Finance,* June 1997.
4. B. Graham, D. Dodd, and C. Tatham, *Security Analysis,* New York, McGraw-Hill, 1951.
5. A. Dewing, *The Financial Policy of Corporations,* New York, The Ronald Press, 1953.
6. Define risk as the contribution that an individual stock makes to the variability of return to a portfolio of which it is a member.
7. If securities are priced fairly, they have zero net present value. Net present value is computed by subtracting the cost of acquiring the investment from the best estimate of the present value of future cash flows to be derived from the investment. For marketable securities, the cost of acquisition is their market price. If the market price is fair and reflects the best estimate, etc., then the net present value is zero. Just as investing in a project with zero net present value has no impact on firm value, so will selling a zero net present value bond to raise capital.

8. This means that every investor in the world uses it.

9. This means that the percentage of your wealth that you can invest in *any* stock can range from minus infinity to plus infinity.

10. For example, early evidence of market overreaction can be found in W. Breen, "Low Price-Earnings Ratios and Industry Relatives," *Financial Analysts Journal,* July–August, 1968; S. Huang, "Study of the Performance of Rapid Growth Stocks," *Financial Analysts Journal,* Jan.–Feb., 1965; F. K. Flugel, "The Rate of Return on High and Low P/E Ratio Stocks," *Financial Analysts Journal,* Nov.–Dec., 1968.

11. M. Roseff and W. Kinney, "Capital Market Seasonality: The Case of Stock Returns," *Journal of Financial Economics,* November 1976.

12. D. Keim, "Size-Related Anomalies and Stock Return Seasonality: Further Empirical Evidence," *Journal of Financial Economics,* June 1983.

13. M. Reinganum, "The Anomalous Behavior of Small Firms in January," *Journal of Financial Economics,* June 1983.

14. M. Gulteken and B. Gulteken, "Stock Market Seasonality: International Evidence," *Journal of Financial Economics,* December 1983.

15. D. Keim, "Dividend Yields and Stock Returns: Implications of Abnormal January Returns," *Journal of Financial Economics,* September 1985.

16. W. DeBondt and R. Thaler, "Does the Stock Market Over-react?" *Journal of Finance,* July 1985.

17. S. Basu, "The Relationship Between Earnings Yield, Market Value and Return for NYSE Common Stocks," *Journal of Financial Economics,* June 1983.

18. J. Lakonishok, A. Shleifer, and R. Vishny, "Contrarian Investment, Extrapolation and Risk," *Journal of Finance,* December 1994.

19. N. Jegadeesh and S. Titman, "Returns to Buying Winners and Selling Losers: Implications for Stock Market Efficiency," *Journal of Finance,* March 1993.

20. T. Loughran and J. Ritter, "The New Issues Puzzle," *Journal of Finance,* March 1995.

21. D. Ikenberry, J. Lakonishok, and T. Vermaelen, "Market Under-reaction to Open Market Share Repurchases," *Journal of Financial Economics,* October/November 1985.

22. R. Haugen, *The New Finance: The Case for an Over-reactive Stock Market,* Prentice Hall, 1998.

PART I

WHAT

2
ESTIMATING EXPECTED RETURN WITH THE THEORIES OF MODERN FINANCE

According to the accepted theories of Modern Finance, differences in risk should be the principal determinant of differences in expected return from one investment to another. At present, the two most popular theories are the Capital Asset Pricing Model (CAPM) and the Arbitrage Pricing Theory (APT).

CAPM works from the assumption that we *all* use Harry Markowitz's optimization tool to build our portfolios. Its predictions are that: (a) the market index, itself, will be one of Harry's efficient portfolios (best possible expected return given its risk), and (b) the only determinant of differences in expected return will be a security's sensitivity to changes in the market's return (market beta).

APT works from the assumption that investors won't allow two risk-free portfolios to exist with different expected returns. If they did, investors would act to eliminate the difference through arbitrage. In fact, this is where APT gets its name. Its prediction is that risk premiums are *proportional* to a security's sensitivity to factors (like interest rates or inflation) that induce correlation in returns across the market.

CAPM

Unlike APT, CAPM makes some pretty strong assumptions, one of which is *absolutely critical* to its predictions.

The critical assumption is that we *all* use Markowitz's optimization in a completely unencumbered fashion. For the theory to work, this assumption must hold *strictly*. It's not sufficient for a few important traders to use Harry's tool, pricing stocks at the margin. We must all be using it—each and every one of us, down to the very last investor.

To see why, consider Figure 2–1A. Here, we plot what you *expect* to get as a return from an investment on the vertical, and *risk* on the horizontal. You may think of risk as either periodic variability in return or the propensity to get something better or worse than what you expect.

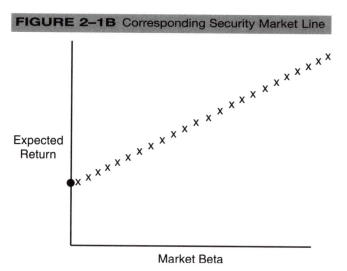

FIGURE 2–1A Market Index on Efficient Set

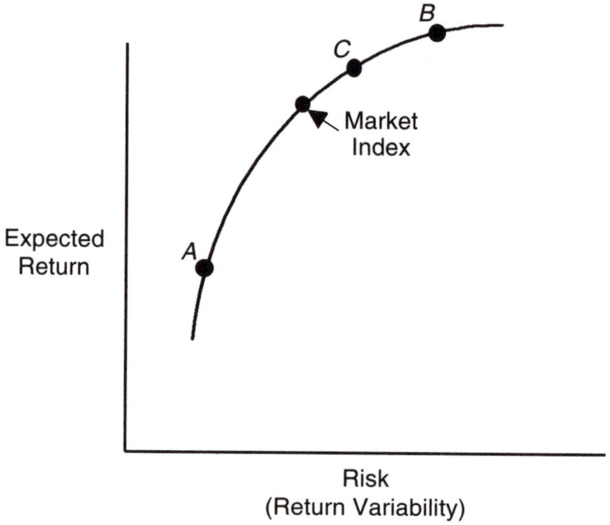

FIGURE 2–1B Corresponding Security Market Line

The curve shown in the figure is called the *efficient set*. As you invest different amounts in different securities, you build different portfolios and you move to different positions in the figure. However, given the nature of the population of securities that are available, you will find it impossible to build a portfolio that lies to the northwest of the curve. The curve is as far as you can go, and is therefore sometimes called the *efficient frontier*. Each point on the frontier shows the position of a different efficient portfolio.

These are the portfolios with the highest possible expected return given their level of risk.

CAPM also makes critical use of what is called a "definitional identity." This is something that is *automatically* true, simply because of the way things have been *defined*.

That is, when he wrote his paper, Harry set forth definitions for things like expected return, variability of return, etc.

Those definitions automatically result in the following truism:

Combinations of efficient portfolios are themselves efficient.

Take two efficient portfolios like *A* and *B* in Figure 2–1A. Suppose I have $20,000 invested in *A* and you have $80,000 invested in *B*. Now, without changing our positions in individual stocks, we combine our investments to form a $100,000 portfolio. A portfolio formed in this way will always be positioned on the efficient set—for example, at point *C*.[1]

CAPM *assumes* that we all find our way to the efficient frontier. Then it makes the following use of the truism:

Think of what you would get if you combined everyone's stockholdings. The combined portfolio would include *all* the outstanding shares of Exxon, General Electric, IBM, etc. The combination would, in fact, *be* the market index.

And, given the truism, if we all hold efficient portfolios, the market index will be efficient as well. This is CAPM's prediction, but note that it gets it with a scant amount of analysis that one would call *economic*.

Some might say that CAPM's most famous prediction is that a security's risk premium rises proportionately with the security's market sensitivity, or beta, as with the individual stocks (the Xs) in Figure 2–1B.

However, another definitional identity tells us that we get a straight line in Figure 2–1B if we estimate a security's sensitivity of return with respect to any portfolio on the efficient set, including portfolios *A, B,* and *C.*

Not just the market index.

So the *real* prediction of CAPM is the *efficiency* of the market index. Given that efficiency, the line[2] of Figure 2–1B follows automatically. In fact, there would be similar lines for any of the efficient portfolios.

Suppose just a few of us decided to hold *inefficient* portfolios inside the efficient frontier. Then we would no longer have the truism working for us. When we combined holdings this time, we would *almost certainly* find an *inefficient* market index, as in Figure 2–2A. And when we consider the positions of securities relative to their sensitivity to the returns to this inefficient market index, *we get the cloud of* Figure 2–2B.

Market beta is no longer the sole determinant of differential expected returns as it is in Figure 2–1B. If the market index is efficient, we get a line as in Figure 2–1B. If it's not, we get a cloud as in Figure 2–2B.

As we will see later in this book, the best evidence indicates that the market index resides deeply inside the efficient set, and the CAPM prediction isn't even close.

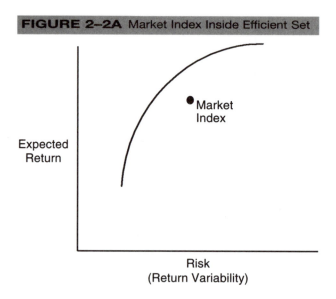

FIGURE 2–2A Market Index Inside Efficient Set

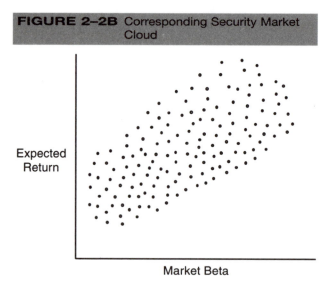

FIGURE 2–2B Corresponding Security Market Cloud

But there are several reasons to dismiss CAPM before even looking at the data.

First, the truism discussed above only works if there are *no* restrictions on our use of Harry's tool.

This means that CAPM only works if we can short-sell any amount of any stock and do anything we want with the proceeds.

Go ahead.

Go to your broker and ask her to lend you one million shares of General Motors. Then sell these shares in the market and receive an amount equal to one million times the price of GM. *Now invest this money in absolutely anything you want.*

Just try it.

Even GM faces restrictions[3] on what it can do with the money it raises by selling its shares!

A typical investor faces limits on the amounts of short sales and is generally restricted to investing the proceeds in cash.

In the face of these restrictions, the truism doesn't hold. Suppose the efficient set of Figure 2–1A was built under these constraints. Suppose also that all investors choose to take positions on this constrained efficient set. If we combine all these portfolios on the efficient set, the market index will still be *inside* the frontier, and we get a cloud similar to that of Figure 2–2B.

But there are several reasons why most investors won't choose to take positions even on the *constrained* efficient set.

For one thing, they may look at risk differently than Harry did when he invented his tool.

In Figures 2–3A and 2–3B, we have drawn two probability distributions for possible monthly returns to two different stock portfolios. We plot the probability of getting a particular return on the vertical axis and the various possible returns on the horizontal axis. Both distributions have about the same expected return and risk (Harry defined risk as variability in possible outcome.), but the distribution of 2–3B is skewed to the right, indicating the distinct possibility of some really big returns. The distribution of 2–3A, on the other hand, is skewed left.

Harry would position the two portfolios at the same point on Figure 2–1A. His tool would treat them as equals, but there is good evidence[4] that most investors would prefer the portfolio on the bottom. Investors with strong preferences for positive skewness would not necessarily be aiming for positions on Harry's efficient set. They may prefer a portfolio inside the frontier because it's positively skewed.

And including their holdings in the market index would help push the index even deeper inside the frontier.

In addition, fiduciaries (people who invest other people's money) are the dominant players in the market. And it seems that fiduciaries care more about their own well-being than about the welfare of their clients.

You see, if the S&P 500 Stock Index fell by 26%, it wouldn't bother most of them much if their client's portfolio fell by 25%. Risk to them is the chance of underperforming, and they measure this risk in terms of tracking error.

Tracking error is the variability in the *differences* between the return to your client's portfolio and the returns to the stock index you're compared with.

FIGURE 2–3A Symmetric Distribution of Possible Returns

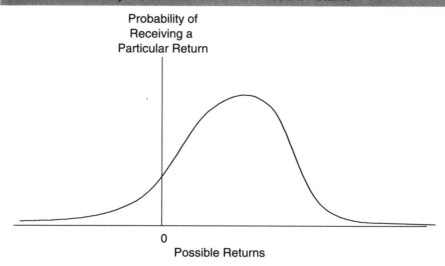

Probability of
Receiving a
Particular Return

0
Possible Returns

FIGURE 2–3B Skewed Distribution of Possible Returns

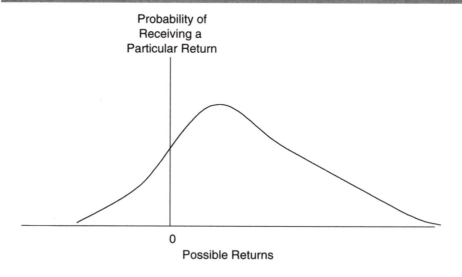

Probability of
Receiving a
Particular Return

0
Possible Returns

You might be able to make a case that some quantitatively oriented, professional investors are making their way toward positions on efficient sets, but their sets are drawn in terms of *tracking error*[5] rather than *variability* of return.

These investors aren't going to help CAPM come true. To them, stocks that have low sensitivity to market return contribute to tracking error in their portfolios to the same degree as do stocks with high sensitivity.

To them, the risk-free asset is the market index itself. Buy it, and you're sure to experience no tracking error whatsoever.

The simple truth is that few, if any, use Harry's tool to manage variability in return. But the theory leans very heavily on the assumption that we *all* do.

Because we don't, we expect CAPM to be a very poor performer when it comes to explaining why different stocks have different returns or, perhaps more important, predicting which stocks will have the biggest future returns.

An important answer to "What?" will *not* be market beta.

APT

To understand APT, we need to discuss the concept of *correlation*.

Let's begin by looking at Figures 2–4A and 2–4B. In 2–4A, we plot the monthly returns[6] to the stock of a small company named Hondo Oil & Gas on the vertical and the returns to another small company named Ben & Jerry's on the horizontal. Each observation represents one of 60 months. For example, in July of 1991, Hondo produced a return of 19.7% and Ben & Jerry's a return of 28.6%.

The line running through the scatter is called a "line of best fit." Suppose you measure the vertical distance of each observation from the line. Then square these distances and add them up. The particular line depicted in 2–4A is the unique line for which this sum is the smallest over all possible straight lines that you can draw through the scatter.

The returns to these two stocks are slightly positively correlated. That means, if Ben & Jerry's realizes a return above its expected value, we would *expect* Hondo to do so as well. It may well not, but nevertheless this is what we would expect.

The correlation between Hondo and Ben & Jerry's is equal to .05. The possible range for this number is between –1.00 and +1.00. If the line of best fit is positively sloped, the correlation is positive. Likewise, a negative slope indicates negative correlation. Correlation approaches either of its extreme values as the fit about the line becomes tighter and tighter. We reach one of the two extremes when the fit is perfect—*all* the observations fall *exactly* on the line.

Figure 2–4B shows a similar scatter plot for two much larger, diversified companies, General Electric (G.E.) and 3M. Note that these larger firms are more highly correlated (.64) and less volatile. This is true in general.

APT assumes that the correlations between stock returns result from the fact that the stocks are responding in similar ways to economic factors, such as changes in interest rates, inflation, or industrial production.

This assumption seems to be reasonable.

Looking at Figures 2–5A and 2–5B, we see how G.E. and 3M respond to percentage changes in long-term government bond yields. Note that when interest rates go higher, the returns to both stocks tend to be lower.

FIGURE 2–4A Scatter Plot of Monthly Returns to Two Small Stocks

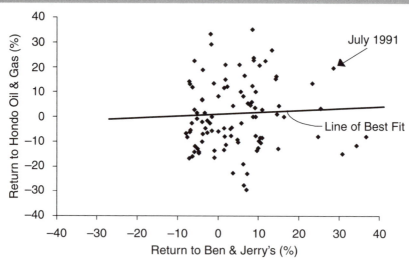

FIGURE 2–4B Scatter Plot of Monthly Returns to Two Large Stocks

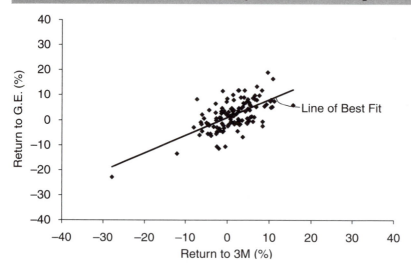

Because both respond similarly to the pull of this common force, movements in interest rates induce positive correlation in the stocks' returns. For example, in April 1987, when interest rates went up, both stocks produced unusually low returns.

The slope of the line of best fit for G.E. is −.53. We shall call this slope G.E.'s *interest-rate beta*. It is a measure of the sensitivity of G.E.'s returns to changes in interest rates.

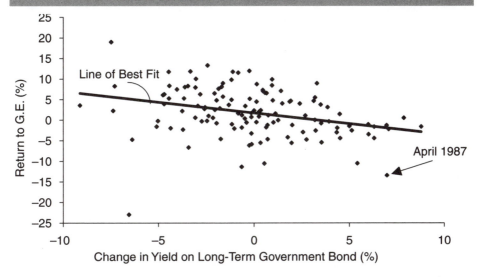

FIGURE 2–5A Relationship between Return to General Electric and Changes in Interest Rates

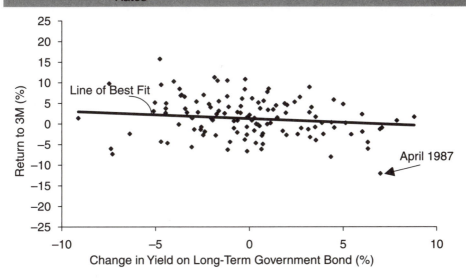

FIGURE 2–5B Relationship between Return to 3M and Changes in Interest Rates

Stocks can have other types of betas as well—inflation betas, oil price betas, etc. Each induces some correlation between stock returns.

APT assumes these factors collectively account for *all* the correlation. Now look at Figure 2–6A. Here we're plotting expected return (as in 2–1A and 2–1B) on the vertical and interest-rate betas for different stocks

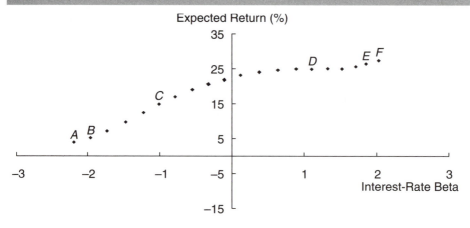

FIGURE 2–6A Curved Relationship between Expected Return and Interest-Rate Beta

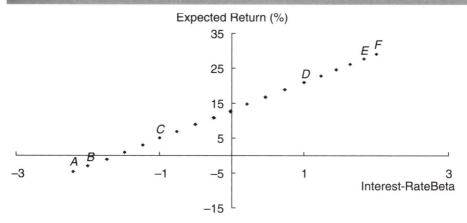

FIGURE 2–6B APT Relationship between Expected Return and Interest-Rate Beta

on the horizontal. Each "diamond" in the figure represents a different stock. Assume there are *many* more stocks than are actually shown in the figure.

Apparently, investors in this market dislike stocks with high interest-rate sensitivity. They require higher expected returns in order to invest in them.

But note that expected returns increase at a *diminishing* rate and that the relationship is somewhat "s" shaped.

APT predicts that this can't happen. If it does, free money is available, and investors will reach for it through a process called *arbitrage*.

It works something like this: We have highlighted six stocks in 2–6A — *A, B, C, D, E,* and *F.* They have the following expected returns and interest-rate betas:

Stock	Expected Return	Interest-Rate Beta
A	4%	–2.20
B	5%	–2.00
C	15%	–1.00
D	25%	+1.00
E	26%	+1.83
F	27%	+2.00

Let's say you build a portfolio where you invest an equal amount in *B* and *F.* The expected return to this portfolio would be the average of 5% and 27%, or 16%. The interest-rate beta would average to zero. Now take some more money and invest 54.54% of it in *E* and 45.46% in *A.* The weighted average expected return is

$$.5454 \times 26\% + .4546 \times 4\% = 16\%.$$

And the interest-rate beta would also average (weighted) to zero.

With lots of stocks out there, you can build a well-diversified portfolio with many of these "pairs," each having a 16% expected return and each having an interest-rate beta of zero.

Assume, for the moment, that the pull of interest rates *alone* accounts for *all* the correlations between *all* of the stocks.[7] You have designed all your pairs to have no response to interest rates. Because this is the only factor that induces correlation, the net returns to the various pairs must then be completely uncorrelated with each other.

In any given month, some of the pairs will produce a return greater than, and some less than, 16%. With many, many pairs, the law of large numbers tells us that the average return across all the pairs must be very, very close to 16%.

For all intents and purposes, you have built a nearly risk-free portfolio with a 16% expected return.

Now let's deal with some of the other available stocks. Suppose, for example, you invest equally in *C* and *D.* Your interest-rate beta will be zero, but this pair will have a 20% expected return.

By going through a process similar to that for the 16% portfolio, you can also build a risk-free portfolio with a 20% expected return.

Now you can arbitrage.

Sell the stocks in the 16% portfolio short. (Borrow shares, and then sell them.) Sell enough to raise $1 million. Now use the $1 million to buy the stocks in the 20% portfolio.

You can expect to lose $160,000 on your short-sales, but you will make $200,000 on the stocks you buy. You pocket the $40,000 difference.

Because there is very little chance of the two portfolios producing returns much different from 16% and 20%, respectively, the $40,000 is virtually guaranteed, and you don't even have to invest any of your own money to get it. The buys are financed with the money obtained by selling the shorts.

Free money.

All because the relationship between expected return and interest sensitivity was *curved.*

If it were *straight,* as it is in Figure 2–6B, there would be no arbitrage opportunities. Here, all zero beta pairs have the same expected return (about 12%).

This, in fact, is the *only* prediction of APT. The relationship between expected return and the various factor sensitivities (betas) must be straight or linear. It can't be curved.

APT doesn't predict which factors are going to be important. It doesn't even tell us if the linear relationships between expected return and the factor betas should be positively sloped (as in 2–6B) or negatively sloped.

It only speaks of linearity.

The assumptions of APT seem reasonable, but the prediction is very weak.

But that is not the real problem.

The *real* operational problem of arbitrage is the reliability of the beta estimates.

Suppose you estimate the interest-rate beta for a stock using the past 60 months of returns, as we did in Figure 2–5A for G.E.

Understand that the beta may have fluctuated over the 60 months. The scatter-plot may reflect the stock's average interest sensitivity only over the total period. But in going forward, what counts is the value for the interest rate beta in the *next month.*

It's going to be very difficult to obtain an unbiased estimate for next month's beta.

The problem is that, in the real market, it is simply impossible to build risk-free portfolios of *risky securities.* They may look risk free over your sample period, but they will not be risk free over the period you actually hold them.

If we can't get a close-to-risk-free portfolio, then trying to exploit any curvature in the relationship between factor betas and expected return becomes problematic at best.

The extra return associated with curvature is likely to be tiny relative to the out-of-sample risk you take in attempting to arbitrage.

The APT arbitrage is an *illusion.* It is a myth.

Talk to any hedge-fund manager.

These guys are the Green Berets of the investment business.

They go long and short, trying to capture spreads in expected returns while trying to minimize variability in the net return.

It's a really tough job.

If you can get variability[8] in the net (long vs. short) return of less than 3%, you're doing a really good job.

When you talk to the "Green Berets," ask them if they ever try to capture spreads by trying to exploit curved relationships, as in 2–6A. You will be lucky to find a single one that does. Most go after the many more bountiful free lunches readily available in the inefficient stock market.

Play the APT game, and you'll first go *hungry* and then go *bust.*

AFTERTHOUGHTS

Market neutral, hedge-fund managers typically short-sell a dollar amount of stocks that is equal to the dollar amount that they invest long in. In any given month, the return to their portfolio is equal to the difference in the returns to the long and short portfolio plus the return obtained by investing the proceeds of the shorts in a risk-free investment like Treasury bills. Fluctuations in the difference in the long and short return (tracking error) really represents the risk of their portfolio. Since they usually like to lever their investment, they want to keep this tracking error as low as possible to protect their equity position.

These managers use risk models to minimize tracking error, while maximizing the spread between the expected returns between the long and short positions. In doing so, they usually make sure that the long and short portfolios have nearly identical positions in individual economic sectors and even in individual industries.

Imagine the efficient set they face, with the expected spread on the vertical and tracking error on the horizontal. Each industry and sector constraint imposed on the set reduces the available expected spread for each level of tracking error. As you go back in time, individual stock sensitivities to things like interest rates and industrial production change from what they are now because the companies may have merged, changed their capital structures, or changed the nature of their products or product line. This means you can't go back very far in time to estimate the betas for your risk model. As a result, betas must be measured with greater imprecision, which increases the real risk of the strategy for each level of expected spread.

Faced with realistic tracking error estimates in excess of 3%, and constrained in terms of their positions in sectors and industries, hedge-fund managers need powerful signals to predict the spreads on the vertical axis of their efficient sets. Curvature in the relationship of Figure 2–6 is simply not going to work for them!

Notes

1. Because portfolio C is 60% invested in portfolio B, it will be positioned in terms of the vertical scale 60% of the distance from A to B.

2. The line of 2–1A is called the Security Market Line in CAPM.

3. To see examples of these restrictions, take a look at a typical bond indenture.

4. Prior to the 1987 crash, a product called portfolio insurance was successfully marketed to institutional investors. It was designed to create positive-skewness portfolio returns. As much as $60 billion in invested capital was covered by portfolio insurance, clearly documenting its great popularity.

5. Tracking error is the volatility of the *differences* between the return on the fiduciary's portfolio and the return to the market index that serves as the fiduciary's benchmark.

6. Return is defined as the sum of dividends paid during the month plus the monthly change in the price of the stock, divided by the price of the stock at the beginning of the month.

7. If other factors account for the correlations, you must then design your portfolio so that it has zero factor betas for each relevant factor. If there is a shortage of stocks with differently signed betas, you must then create your pairs by going short in one and long in the other.

8. Standard deviation.

3

ESTIMATING PORTFOLIO RISK AND EXPECTED RETURN WITH AD HOC FACTOR MODELS

Figure 3–1 shows the probability distribution of rates of return to a stock portfolio. While it would be nice to be able to actually see the distribution of possible returns to the portfolio we're going to be investing in, we can't.

Nevertheless, when you invest in a group of stocks, given their nature, there are underlying probabilities associated with the appearance of different returns.

When you buy a lottery ticket, you don't know how tickets have been sold, only that they have been. And there is an underlying distribution for the game.

While we can't see the entire distribution for stock returns, we do have the tools to give us estimates of two of its characteristics. We can use *expected-return factor models* to estimate the expected return (as indicated by the

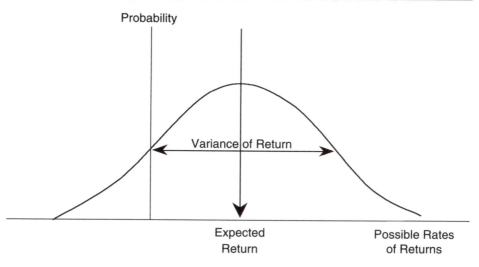

FIGURE 3–1 Probability Distribution for Returns to a Portfolio

vertical arrow in Figure 3–1) and *risk factor models* to estimate the possible variability or variance in return (as indicated by the horizontal arrow).

These *ad hoc* risk and expected-return factor models are not based on any theory. They are purely statistical in nature. And, as you will see in the chapters that follow, the factor models (at least the expected-return varieties) are nearly as *powerful* in their predictive power as financial theory is *weak* in its predictive power.

We will first discuss risk models, and then turn our attention to the relatively more powerful expected-return models.

RISK FACTOR MODELS

General Electric returns go up by 6% in a month in which it pays no dividend.

Why?

There are many reasons, each contributing one component to this total rate of return.

Perhaps there was a decline in long-term bond yields during the month and G.E. responded positively in accord with the slope of the line of Figure 2–5A. In fact, the return would have been even better had it not been for the possibility that inflation had been higher than expected. You see, G.E. also has a negative inflation beta.

In the month, other changes in the macroeconomy added their components to G.E.'s return and to the return of other stocks as well. Different stocks tend to have betas of the same sign against the various factors coming from the macroeconomy. So the components induced by these macrofactors cause stock prices to move somewhat in tandem.

But they can induce negative correlation as well. Another firm might have a great deal of long-term debt in its capital structure. The decline in interest rates increased the market value of that debt. Given that the market value of the company's total assets remains constant, the market value of its common stock (the difference between the market values of assets and debt) must fall. This firm would have a positively sloped line of best fit in Figure 2–5A.

The 6% return for G.E. also contained a component that was *idiosyncratic* to the company, a component that affected only G.E. and no other firm.

Perhaps the company discovered and patented a promising new product. A key person in the firm may have died. A fire or a strike may have occurred.

We call the component of the return caused by events like these idiosyncratic or *diversifiable*. If you invest in lots of stocks, some will have good idiosyncratic things happen to them, and some bad. The more stocks you buy, the more you can count on the fact that the good and bad will be about evenly distributed. If so, in aggregate, they will have little influence on the portfolio's monthly return. Thus, the impact of these idiosyncratic components is diversifiable.

We call the components in the return caused by macroevents systematic or *nondiversifiable*. Because stocks usually have uniformly signed betas against these factors, you can't count on evenly distributed (positive or negative) responses, no matter how many stocks you buy.

Because there are so many stocks in the market index, the index is nearly unaffected by truly idiosyncratic events. It's the systematic events that send it up and down.

For any stock or portfolio, we can divide the variability or *variance* of its return into these two parts: systematic risk and diversifiable risk.

Return Variance = Systematic Risk + Diversifiable Risk

To keep things simple, this time assume that inflation and oil prices are the only factors that induce a correlation between stock returns.

To compute systematic risk of a portfolio with a risk factor model, you interface the correlations between the various macrofactors with the portfolio's factor betas using the matrix of Table 3–1.

The four elements inside the matrix are correlations[1] between the two factors. (The correlation between anything and itself is 1.00.) The elements alongside and atop the matrix are the portfolio betas (the slopes of lines like that of Figure 2–5A and 2–5B) with respect to the two factors.

Figure 3–2 shows a scatter plot of the rate of inflation against percentage changes in the price of oil. The correlation is equal to .22. This is the number that would go inside the matrix (at the upper right and lower left).

But how do we get the betas for the portfolio?

A given percentage of the portfolio is invested in each of several stocks. These percentages are called portfolio weights. To compute the portfolio's beta, you compute the weighted average of the betas across all the stocks in the portfolio. Recall Figure 2–6A: We take a weighted average in the same way.

But how do you compute the betas for the individual stocks? By performing an analysis similar to that of Figure 2–5A and 2–5B.

Now that we know where the betas and correlations come from, how do we actually compute systematic risk?

Table 3–1 Spreadsheet for Computing Systematic Risk

	Portfolio Beta (Inflation)	*Portfolio Beta (Oil Price)*
Portfolio beta (inflation)	1.00	Correlation between inflation and oil price
Portfolio beta (oil price)	Correlation between inflation and oil price	1.00

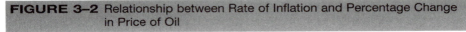

FIGURE 3–2 Relationship between Rate of Inflation and Percentage Change in Price of Oil

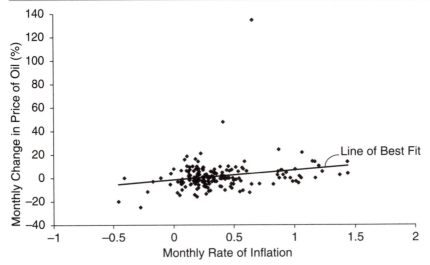

Simply by multiplying each element inside the matrix (Table 3–2) by the beta directly at the side of the matrix, and then multiplying this product by the beta directly at the top. Do this for each element in the matrix to get four products. Then, add them up to get the systematic risk as in Table 3–2.

With more macrofactors the matrix gets bigger, but the process remains the same. With three factors, the matrix is 3 by 3, and you add up nine products. With four, it's 4 by 4, and you add up 16. And so on.

What macrofactors should you use? That question's not completely settled, but the following list[2] seems to be a pretty good one:

- The rate of inflation[3]
- The rate of change in industrial production
- The difference in the rate of return between a long- and short-term U.S. Government bonds
- The difference between the rate of return between long-term, low-grade, corporate bonds and long-term U.S. Government bonds[4]
- The rate of change in the price of oil

Usually, the factors used in a risk model are *changes* in variables. In contrast, as we will see in the next section, *levels* of variables are usually used in an expected-return factor model.

In picking factors for a risk model, your goal is to find those that best account for the correlations between stock returns.

Table 3–2 Computing Portfolio Systematic Risk

	Portfolio beta (inflation)	×	Portfolio beta (inflation)	×	1.00
+	Portfolio beta (inflation)	×	Portfolio beta (oil price)	×	Correlation between inflation and oil price
+	Portfolio beta (oil price)	×	Portfolio beta (oil price)	×	1.00
+	Portfolio beta (inflation)	×	Portfolio beta (oil price)	×	Correlation between inflation and oil price
=	Portfolio Systematic Risk			

If you have chosen a good list, the idiosyncratic components of the returns that are left will be uncorrelated from one stock to the next. If you find they are not, you must choose better factors.

Now that we have learned how to compute systematic risk, let's move on to computing diversifiable risk.

Figure 3–3 shows how truly diversifiable risk should behave as you include more stocks in an equally-weighted stock portfolio. We plot diversifiable risk on the vertical axis and the number of stocks in the portfolio on the horizontal. The graph assumes that each stock added has the same level of diversifiable risk. Note that as you add more and more stocks, diversifiable risk approaches zero.

FIGURE 3–3 Diversifiable Risk Decreases with Number of Stocks in Portfolio

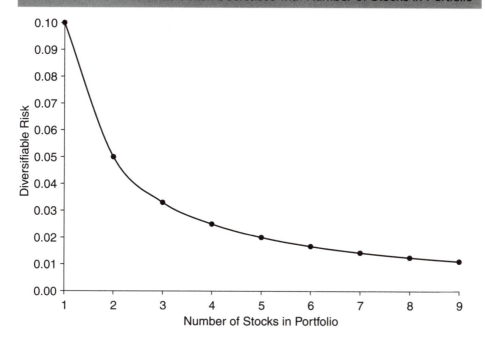

Think of the curve of Figure 3–3 as a glide path. If your glide path looks like this one, you have done a good job in selecting factors. The ones you selected truly account for the return correlations between stocks. If your glide path comes down more slowly, the idiosyncratic components of return are positively correlated across different stocks. If it comes down more quickly, they're negatively correlated. In either case, you need to select your macrofactors more carefully.

With a good set of factors, if you invest an equal amount in each stock, the diversifiable risk of the portfolio can be approximated by the following ratio:[5]

$$\frac{\text{The Average Diversifiable Risk of Each Stock}}{\text{The Number of Stocks in the Portfolio}}$$

By adding your estimate of diversifiable risk to your estimate of systematic risk, you now have an estimate of the risk or variability of the portfolio.

How good is this estimate?

Mark Fedinia, a professor at the University of Wisconsin, performed some experiments that will give us a good idea.

For each year from 1963 through 1994, Fedina picked 100 stocks at random from those listed on the New York Stock Exchange (NYSE).[6] He then asked, "Suppose I want to invest in the lowest-volatility portfolio possible for the next 12 months. How should I allocate my funds to the 100 stocks so as to achieve this result?"

To find out, Fedinia used, as data, the 60 preceding monthly returns for the stocks. Given a particular fund allocation, Fedinia calculated the volatility of the portfolio in two ways.

First, he made a naïve estimate. Fedinia assumed that the volatility in the next year would be the portfolio's average volatility over the trailing five years.[7] Then he used Harry's optimizer to find the funds allocation with the lowest trailing five-year volatility. Volatility in the *next* year was then calculated for this allocation. Fedinia repeated this experiment 270 times for each year.

The average volatility achieved (in the next year) over all years (1963–1994) was 12.32%.

Then Fedinia used a factor model to make the volatility estimate. He used a statistical procedure to find five factors that fully explained the correlations between the returns to the NYSE stock population. In Fedinia's case, the factors were not economic variables like the rate of inflation. Rather, they were portfolios of stocks.

To get his volatility estimate, he separately estimated the systematic and diversifiable risk. Then he added them and took the square root to get the volatility estimate.

Other than the means by which volatility is computed, the nature of the experiment was exactly the same as with the naïve estimate.

Under the factor model, the average volatility achieved was 11.93%.

While this *is* an improvement over the naïve estimate, it's only a modest improvement.

As we shall see, the real power of factor models comes in estimating *expected return*.

And we will learn about expected-return factor models next.

EXPECTED-RETURN FACTOR MODELS

With a risk-factor model, you are looking for factors that are able to account for the correlations between stock returns.

Correlation is a co-movement between stocks.

Thus, in a risk model, the factors used are generally things that *move*, such as inflation, industrial production, and oil prices.

In an expected-return model, you will use factors that help explain and predict which stocks have tended to, and will continue to, drift up or down in value relative to others. These factors tend to be individual stock characteristics, which differ in *level* from one stock to another.

Things like the ratio of the accounting book value of a firm's equity capital to the total market value of the firm's common stock—the book-to-price ratio.

Figure 3–4 plots the rate of return in the month of January 1981 on its vertical axis and book-to-price ratio going into the month on the horizon-

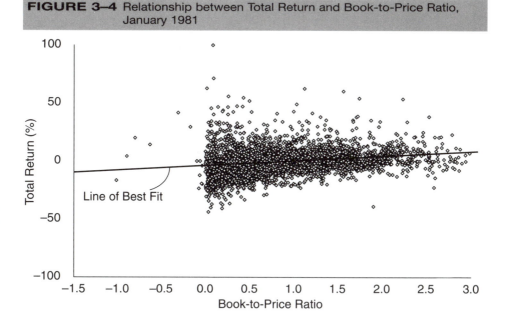

FIGURE 3–4 Relationship between Total Return and Book-to-Price Ratio, January 1981

tal axis. The dots in the figure are roughly the 3,000 largest stocks in the United States. The line going through the scatter is another line of best fit. With the exception of a few stocks, book-to-price ratio is truncated at zero because book values are seldom negative.

The line is positively sloped. In this month, the stocks with larger book-to-price ratios tended to have higher rates of return. In this month, book-to-price had a positive *payoff.*

The payoff to book-to-price will vary from month to month. Each month will have a different scatter plot. Mostly, the payoff is positive, but there are also many months when it's negative.

In any case, the book-to-price factor helps us to explain why different stocks produced different returns in any given month, such as January 1981.

Other factors will also be useful. The first step in building an expected-return factor model is finding a list of factors that adequately describes the profile of a stock and its company. Your list may be long. Remember, we're dealing with a highly inefficient market. The aspects of the corporate profile that are relevant to forecasting expected returns aren't limited to risk. They may include measures of cheapness or dearness in market price (such as book-to-price), profitability, insider trading activity, etc.

For each month, you estimate the payoff to each factor simultaneously, using a statistical method called *multiple regression.*

Imagine a *three-dimensional* Figure 3–4, where you have *two* horizontal axes—one for book-to-price ratio and another for, say, firm size. Return is once again plotted on the vertical scale.

You're probably sitting in a room right now. Hopefully it has a corner. Look at the corner, and try to visualize the three-dimensional graph. Try hard, because we're going to be using this visual to help us understand something important later in the book.

The two horizontal axes (book-to-price ratio and size) are plotted along the edges of the floor at the bottom of the walls. The vertical axis (total return) goes from floor to ceiling along the corner.

Now think of a plot point, representing one stock, in this three-dimensional graph. It floats above the floor, away from the corner. The distance from the floor to the plot point is the stock's return for the month. Directly below the plot point, mark a point on the floor. If you move directly from that point to the left wall, you will see the stock's book-to-price ratio. Move from the point directly to the right wall to see the firm's size.

Now imagine a thousand plot points in the room.

This time, we pass a *plane* of best fit through the plot points. This unique plane is the one that minimizes the *sum* of the squared vertical distances between each plot point and the plane itself. The slope of the plane *along each wall* provides simultaneous estimates of the payoffs to book-to-price ratio and size.

That's what goes on in a multiple regression.

We can't visualize what's happening in a three-factor regression, but the same basic process goes on as with two, and so on with four, and through as many factors as you choose to use.

Calculate these regressions over a number of past months to obtain a history of the payoffs to the various factors in your model. Then, based on that history and a statistical estimation process, you can obtain an *expected payoff* for the *next* month.

Your expectation may simply be the mean value for the payoff throughout the history. It may be a rolling mean over the last few months. It may be a weighted mean, where the more-recent monthly payoffs are weighted more heavily. You might even project next month's payoff with a statistical time-series model.

You then interface your projected *payoff* with each stock's *exposure* to that particular factor.

Payoff—the slope of the line as in Figure 3–4.
Exposure—the book-to-price ratio for any stock in the figure as given on the horizontal axis.

We have payoffs and exposures in *risk models* as well.

Payoff—the monthly rate of growth in industrial production.
Exposure—the stock's industrial production beta.

In estimating expected return with a factor model, you use a spreadsheet that looks something like the one in Table 3–3.

In this spreadsheet, factor exposures are expressed as the number of standard deviations[8] a stock is from an average stock's factor exposure. Thus, we see that the XYZ Corporation's stock is selling at a book-to-price ratio that is 2.5 standard deviations above the cross-sectional average. Based on some means of projecting from the past history of the payoffs to book-to-price, we project a payoff to book-to-price that is .2% (20 basis points) per unit of standard deviation. Multiplying the exposure by the expected payoff, we obtain a component of total expected return that's coming from the stock's book-to-price ratio of .5%.

Table 3–3 Spreadsheet for Computing Expected Return for XYZ Stock

Factor	Exposure	×	Projected Payoff	=	Return Component
Book/price	2.5 S.D.		.2%		.5%
Size	3.0 S.D.		–.3%		–.9%
•	•		•		•
•	•		•		•
•	•		•		•
Debt/equity	–1.0 S.D.		–.2%		.2%
Total expected return relative to an average stock:					3%

After finding the components of expected return coming from the other factors (including the many that are not expressly shown), you total the components to get the difference between this stock's expected return and the expected return of an average stock (a stock with a zero exposure to each factor).

Thus, while a risk model interfaces factor exposures (macrofactor betas) with the *correlation matrix* of factor payoffs (inflation, industrial production, etc.), an expected-return model interfaces factor exposures (book-to-price, size, etc.) with the *expected values* of factor payoffs.

Of the two types of models, risk models are far more popular with professional investors.[9]

This book focuses on the vastly underappreciated expected-return model.

As shown above, the predictions of a risk model are slightly more accurate than the naïve prediction that the portfolio will be as risky in the future as it was in the past.

The comparable naïve prediction for an expected-return model is that the portfolio will have a return in the future equal to its average return in the past. As we shall see later, the naïve model doesn't even come close to an expected-return factor model in its predictive power.

The power of an expected-return model is largely unappreciated because, in the past, the list of factors used in the model has been limited to those predicted as useful by the theories of Modern Finance. The real determinants of expected return go well beyond those predicted by APT and CAPM. These factors will be developed in the chapters that follow.

AFTERTHOUGHTS

Suppose someone asked you to design risk and expected-return factor models for the stock markets of Europe. In selecting the factors for your risk model, would you use the macroeconomic variables (such as interest rates and industrial production) from each country, or would you use weighted average numbers from the European Community? Since what happens in the United States and in U.S. financial markets seems to greatly impact markets abroad, might it be a good idea to include macroeconomic numbers from the United States in your model? Might exchange rates play a more important role in a European model than they would in a U.S. model? Would you use the exchange rate between the Euro and the dollar or the exchange rates between the individual countries in Europe? How would the move toward a common currency over time create problems for your estimation?

In designing your expected return model, would you model the countries individually or across all of Europe? If you choose individually, how would you handle countries like Holland where the market is dominated by just a few stocks? Eventually, modeling individual countries in Europe might be as silly as modeling individual states in the United States. How would you know when that time had come?

Notes

1. We assume that the macrofactors have been transformed statistically to have a standard deviation of 1.00.
2. Some of these factors were originally suggested by N. Chen, S. Ross, and R. Roll, "Economic Forces and the Stock Market," *Journal of Business,* 1986.
3. Some use unexpected changes in inflation, industrial production, and the price of oil, because they believe that an efficient market will react only to unexpected changes in the factors. Expected changes are usually based on the predictions of statistical models. However, given the gross level of inefficiencies in the market, you will find that it makes little difference in predictive power whether you use raw changes or unexpected changes.
4. This factor reflects changes in investor confidence. When low-grade corporate bonds outperform, it's because investors have revised their estimate of the probability of default downward.

5. In the more general case, if you have properly accounted for the correlations between the returns to different stocks, the diversifiable risk of a portfolio of stocks is equal to the sum of the product of the squared percentage invested in each stock and the diversifiable risk of each stock.
6. To be eligible, a stock must have the returns data required for the test.
7. Assuming that the portfolio is rebalanced monthly to keep the funds allocation constant.
8. Compute the mean value for the factor across all the stocks in your population. Then, for each stock, compute the difference between the stock's factor exposure and the mean. Square each of these differences. Add them up. Divide the sum by the number of stocks. Now take the square root. That is the cross-sectional standard deviation.
9. Barra Inc. is currently the chief supplier of *risk* models in the investment business.

4
PAYOFFS TO THE FIVE FAMILIES

HOW MANY FACTORS?

Finance professors like to smile knowingly (or even laugh up their sleeves) when they come upon a factor model like the one we just described, in which more than 50 factors are used to estimate the expected rates of return for stocks.

They smile because they think they know that the market is efficient, and given *this* belief, they also believe that the only determinant of differences in expected return will be risk. If they are friends of CAPM, they believe in a single determinant of differences in expected return—market beta. If they are friends of APT, they may believe in more than one beta, but the number is limited to the number of factors needed to fully account for the correlations between stock returns. Nearly all of them agree that this number is far less than 50, so anyone who would use such a large number must surely be a fool.

However, even in an efficient market, the determinants of expected stock returns aren't going to be purely risk-related.

First, we have *taxes*.

Municipal bonds have lower expected returns than do corporate bonds, even if they have the same risk and maturity. That's because municipals are tax-sheltered. So they sell at premium prices and have lower pretax expected returns so that their after-tax expected return is commensurate with that of the corporate bonds.

Are common stocks differentially exposed to taxes?

The answer is yes. Some firms write big dividend checks to their stockholders. The IRS takes a significant bite out of these checks.

Other firms reinvest most of their profits in investment projects. Still others have stock repurchase programs, where they buy their own stock through tender offers or in the marketplace. For both types of firms, stockholders receive their return more as price appreciation than as dividend income.

Capital gains are deferred until realized, and, even then, they are often taxed at lower rates.

Firms that write big dividend checks expose their investors to the IRS. Their stockholders should require higher expected returns to make after-tax returns commensurate with firms that don't.

Tax premiums in expected returns.

Second, we have differential *liquidity*.

It costs money to trade stocks. First, you must pay commissions to the brokers who trade the shares. The broker executes the trades with specialists, or dealers. They make money by buying the stocks from people who want to sell at a bid price and selling stock to people who want to buy at a higher-asked price. The difference is called the bid-asked spread. If you buy the stock now (at the asked price) and sell later (at the bid), you contribute the spread to the dealer. This is how dealers make their living.

This bid-asked spread is a second component of the cost of trading.

Some stocks are traded less frequently than others. To make a given amount of money over a given period of time, dealers must widen the spread on these stocks, making them more costly to trade.

Dealers typically hold smaller inventories of infrequently traded stocks. If you're a large investor and want to hold a significant position in an infrequently traded stock, you may find that your attempt to buy is affecting the price. Your bid may, in fact, significantly deplete the dealer's inventory in the stock, and, to restore it, the dealer may raise the bid.

This third component of trading cost is called *market impact*.

Given their nature, stocks may have differential commissions, spreads, and potential market impact. Furthermore, multiple aspects of a corporation's profile (such as size, risk, and institutional ownership) may determine total expected trading costs.

In any case, even in an efficient market, investors will want higher expected returns on stocks that are expected to be more costly to trade. And they may base their expectations about trading costs on various facets of the corporate profile.

Finally, we have market *inefficiency*.

Errors in market pricing open the door to a *myriad* of predictive factors—insider trading activity, earnings surprises, measures of cheapness in price—all of which may be critically important in predicting future stock returns.

The efficient markets people should stop laughing until they can predict as well with their financial theories as we can with our *ad hoc* expected-return factor models!

THE FAMILIES

For purposes of the expected-return factor model described in this book, we shall divide the factors used into five groups or families.

This is not to imply that these five are the only families useful in predicting stock returns. Other families, including analysts' earnings estimate revisions, unexpected earnings reports, measures of insider trading activity, membership in stock indices, stockholder demography, corporate repurchase and sale of shares may also prove very useful.

The five families singled out here are nonproprietary, because they are included in a factor model that is in the public domain.[1]

RISK FACTORS

The first family that we will consider is *risk*—the family most finance professors would easily consider to be most important.

Actually, it turns out to be *least* important. And any importance it has is apparently *perverse*. Over the long-term, most risky stocks have actually tended to produce lower rates of return.

Our risk family will include factors predicted to be important by CAPM and APT. Thus, we include market beta and sensitivities of stock return to various numbers coming from the financial markets and the macroeconomy.

However, since we have very little regard for either of these theories, we will want to employ a more comprehensive list of risk measures. The complete list of risk-family members includes the following:

- Market Beta (trailing a 60-month regression of monthly excess returns)
- APT Betas (trailing a 60-month regression on Treasury bill returns, percentage changes in industrial production, the rate of inflation, the difference in the returns to long- and short-term government bonds, and the difference in the returns to corporate and government bonds)
- Volatility of Total Return (trailing 60 months)
- Residual Variance (nonmarket-related risk over trailing 60 months)
- Earnings Risk (standard error of year-over-year earnings per share about time trend)
- Debt-to-Equity Ratio (most recently available book value of total debt to book value of common equity)
- Debt-to-Equity Trend (five-year trailing time trend in debt-to-equity ratio)
- Times Interest Earned (net operating income to total interest charges)
- Times Interest Earned Trend (five-year quarterly time trend in year-over-year times interest earned)
- Yield Variability (five-year trailing volatility in earnings, dividend, and cash flow yield)

LIQUIDITY FACTORS

As we discussed previously, some stocks are more costly to trade than others. Some professors fantasize that liquidity differences don't affect stock prices. If they did, investors would try to capture the premium returns to the less liquid stocks by trading them slowly and patiently to avoid having their trades affect the prices of the stocks. However, they would still have to face a higher bid-asked spread, and, although many investors are willing to trade patiently, even more are not. Consequently, we include a family of *liquidity factors,* which include the following members:

- Market Capitalization (current market price times the most recently available number of shares outstanding)
- Market Price per Share
- Trading Volume/Market Capitalization (trailing 12-month average monthly trading volume to market capitalization)
- Trading Volume Trend (five-year time trend in monthly trading volume)

MEASURES OF CHEAPNESS

Some firms are currently prospering, while others are suffering.

Competition will eventually bring a halt to both. The profitable firm will face the entry of competitors, which will lower prices and take customers. Conversely, the unprofitable firm will see competitors leave and reinvent themselves in other lines of business. They will then be able to raise prices and take their former competitors' clients, ending their suffering.

How long, on average, will the process of competitive entry and exit take?

We know it takes different amounts of time in different product lines. There are obviously differential barriers to competition in different industries.

But how long, on average? And does the stock market know how long?

For the sake of argument, suppose it takes about *five* years, on average.

If, however, the market prices stocks on the presumption that it takes *ten* years, then it will set the price of the profitable firm too high, believing its prosperity will stick around longer than it actually will. Likewise, the price of the unprofitable firm will be too low, for it will recover faster than the market believes.

Prosperity brings growth. The market will expect that future profits will be larger than present ones. Thus, the profitable firm will have a current market price that is high relative to its current level of profits, or expensive.

If the market guesses ten and it's really five, the price is too expensive. The market will be disappointed in the quality of future earnings reports and future returns will be low.

Suffering inhibits growth and may even bring decline. Thus, the unprofitable firm will have a current market price that is lower relative to its current level of profits, and the stock will be selling cheap in the market.

If the market guesses ten and in reality it is actually five, cheap stocks are bargains. The quality-of-earnings reports beyond five years will be surprisingly good. Future returns to currently cheap stocks will tend to be high.

Suppose, instead, it actually takes five years and the market guesses *three*. Now, because its prosperity will continue longer than the market believes, the relatively expensive and profitable firm is the bargain. Expensive stocks will tend to produce the greater returns in the future.

We have great confidence that the inefficient market *doesn't* get it exactly right.

If it doesn't, there will be significant (positive or negative) payoffs to measures of *cheapness*.

Changes in market perceptions regarding the speed of competitive entry can also influence the payoffs to cheap and expensive stocks. Suppose it is again actually five years, but the market gradually revises its perception from ten to fifteen years. During the period of change, expensive stocks will produce relatively high returns. A longer period of perceived prosperity justifies a higher price.

Thus, even if the perceived period of competitive entry is, in general, longer than is true, there may be relatively brief periods of positive payoffs to expensive stocks as the market goes through transitions in its perceptions.

Thus, a variety of measures of cheapness constitutes our third factor family.

Why a variety?

Because a single measure may not reveal the true picture. Take an unprofitable firm. Its earnings may have fallen to only a few cents a share. It may appear expensive if you compare its earnings to its price, but if you look at the ratio of its sales (per share) to its price or its book value to its price, the stock will seem to be selling cheap in the market.

Our cheapness family includes the following measures:

- Earnings-to-Price Ratio (most recently available four-quarters earnings to current market price)
- Earnings-to-Price Trend (five-year monthly time trend in earnings-to-price ratio)
- Book-to-Price Ratio (most recently available book value to current market price)
- Book-to-Price Trend (five-year monthly time trend in book-to-price ratio)
- Dividend-to-Price Ratio (most recently available four-quarters dividend to current market price)
- Dividend-to-Price Trend (five-year monthly time trend in dividend-to-price ratio)
- Cash Flow-to-Price Ratio (most recently available ratio of earnings plus depreciation per share to current market price)

- Cash Flow-to-Price Trend (five-year monthly time trend in cash-flow-to-price ratio)
- Sales-to-Price Ratio (most recently available four-quarters total sales per share to current market price)
- Sales-to-Price Trend (five-year monthly time trend in sales-to-price ratio)

MEASURES OF PROFITABILITY

As we will extensively discuss in Part II of this book, the market prices with great *imprecision*. This means that it assigns different prices to stocks with the same future profit potential and the same price to other stocks with different future profit potentials.

Given that two stocks are selling at identical levels of cheapness, our intuition tells us that the more profitable of the two companies will have the better outlook for future return.

The payoff to cheapness can be positive or negative, depending on whether the market overestimates or underestimates the length of the mean reversion in profitability.

On the other hand, the payoff to measures of profitability must be either zero (if the market prices with perfect precision) or positive (if the market prices with imprecision).

The greater the degree of imprecision, the larger the payoff to profitability.

Let the members of the profitability family come forward:

- Profit Margin (net operating income to total sales)
- Profit Margin Trend (trailing five-year quarterly time trend in year-over-year profit margin)
- Capital Turnover (total sales to total assets)
- Capital Turnover Trend (trailing five-year quarterly time trend in year-over-year capital turnover)
- Return on Assets (net operating income to total assets)
- Return on Assets Trend (trailing five-year quarterly time trend in year-over-year return on assets)
- Return on Equity (net income to total book value of total equity capital)
- Return on Equity Trend (trailing five-year quarterly time trend in year-over-year return on equity)
- Earnings Growth (trailing five-year quarterly time trend in year-over-year earnings per share divided by the trailing five-year average earnings per share)
- Earnings Surprise (the percentage difference between reported earnings and projected earnings for the most recent earnings report)

TECHNICAL FACTORS

Finance professors have spent a great deal of time ridiculing chartists.

Chartists like to plot (in various ways) the history of stock prices on graphs. By analyzing their graphs, chartists believe they can project future prices and make money.

Finance professors believe that stock prices reflect all information at all times. Stock prices move only in response to new, unexpected information that, by its nature, is completely unpredictable. In the efficient market, the response to new information should be instant and accurate. By its very nature, completely unpredictable information must come to the market in a random fashion. Therefore, the instant and accurate response of stock prices must be random as well.

In this context, changes in stock prices (like the new information) will also be unpredictable.

Don't you understand? The chartists are simply *wasting* their time, say the professors.

But, just in case the professors are wrong, we will include a family of factors that describe the performance of a stock price over various periods in the past. The members of the *technical* fifth family include the following:

- Excess Return (relative to the S&P 500) in Previous 1 Month
- Excess Return (relative to the S&P 500) in Previous 2 Months
- Excess Return (relative to the S&P 500) in Previous 3 Months
- Excess Return (relative to the S&P 500) in Previous 6 Months
- Excess Return (relative to the S&P 500) in Previous 12 Months
- Excess Return (relative to the S&P 500) in Previous 24 Months
- Excess Return (relative to the S&P 500) in Previous 60 Months

SECTOR FACTORS

Finally, we include a set of ten sector factors. If a stock has its principle line of business in a particular sector, the sector factor takes on a value of 1.00; if not, the sector factor takes a value of 0.00.

The payoff to the sector factors can be interpreted as the monthly return to the sector, after allowing for the influence of all the other factors presented previously.

The sectors included are:

- Durable goods
- Nondurable goods
- Utilities
- Energy
- Construction
- Business equipment

- Manufacturing
- Transportation
- Financial
- Business services

THE PAYOFFS

Please take another look at Figure 3–4.

This is a single-factor regression, where we are estimating the payoff to book-to-price in the month of January 1990. The slope of the line (.04) is the payoff for the month.

We now move to a multiple-factor regression (like the corner of the room). We *simultaneously* estimate the payoffs to *all* the factors listed above in each of the months from 1979 through 1999.

Our stock population will roughly be the largest 3500 U.S. stocks during the 1980 to 2000 period.

Over the period 1979–99, we estimate 252 payoffs for each factor, and then take an average over the 21 years.[2]

The larger this average, and the smaller the monthly variability of the payoff, the more confident we are that the true, underlying expected value of the payoff to the factor is actually different from zero.

The factors are ranked with respect to the confidence (or probability) with which we can say that the true expected values of the payoffs are actually different from zero.

The extreme left-hand panels of Table 4–1 show the average values for the payoffs to the 12 most important (nonsector) factors over the 1979–99 period. Also shown are the probabilities that the underlying expected return to each factor is truly nonzero.

In interpreting these numbers, remember that each payoff is the increase or decrease in expected monthly return associated with a one-standard-deviation change in a stock's exposure to a particular factor.

To illustrate, let's consider the book-to-price factor. Suppose there are two stocks. One stock has an earnings-to-price ratio that is exactly equal to the average earnings-to-price across the 3,500 stocks. The second stock has an earnings-to-price ratio that is one standard deviation greater than average. Let's also say that the two stocks are identical in every other respect. Based on the mean payoff for the first half of the period, we would say that the second stock has an expected return that is .18% (or 18 basis points) higher than the first stock.

With this in mind, let's examine the pattern of the payoffs over the total first half period.

Start with the chartists, who may be on to something after all. Four of the ten are related to the historic performance of a firm's stock price. We see negative payoffs to recent performance. If the relative performance

Table 4–1 Mean and Confidence Levels for the Most Important Factors of 1979–1999

Factor	Total Period 1979/01 through 1999/12		First Half 1979/01 through 1989/06		Second Half 1989/07 through 1999/12		Since Original Study 1994/01 through 1999/12	
	Mean	*Confidence*	*Mean*	*Confidence*	*Mean*	*Confidence*	*Mean*	*Confidence*
1-month excess return	−0.10%	99%	−0.65%	99%	−0.76%	99%	−0.88%	99%
12-month excess return	0.38	99	0.34	99	0.43	99	0.36	99
2-month excess return	−0.20	99	−0.16	99	−0.22	99	−0.38	99
Trading volume trend	0.10	99	0.08	99	0.09	99	0.18	99
Earnings-to-price ratio	0.18	99	0.19	99	0.16	99	0.25	99
Cash flow-to-price ratio	0.14	99	0.21	99	0.08	92	0.08	83
Return on equity	0.15	99	0.08	76	0.21	99	0.18	99
Cash flow/price variability	−0.10	99	−0.15	99	−0.05	84	−0.05	70
6-month excess return	−0.14	99	−0.06	50	−0.21	99	−0.21	95
Return on assets	0.10	99	0.09	80	0.10	94	0.08	78
Payout ratio	−0.06	96	−0.05	73	−0.07	95	−0.12	94
Trading volume/market cap	−0.04	91	−0.02	36	−0.07	98	−0.07	94

was strong in the past one-to-six months, you should expect weakness in the next month, or *short-term reversal* pattern in stock returns.

We also see evidence of *intermediate-term momentum.* A strong stock performance in the previous six-to-twelve months bodes for a good performance next month.

Finally, while they didn't make the top twelve, there is also evidence of significant *long-term reversal* patterns in stock returns. If a stock's performance has been strong in the past three-to-five years, that bodes ill for the following month.

What about measures of cheapness? Does the market overestimate or underestimate the length of time it takes profitability to mean-revert to normal levels?

Two cheapness factors make the top twelve—the ratios of earnings, and cash flow to price.

As we discussed above, the positive payoffs to these factors are consistent with the market *overestimating* the length of time it takes competition to force profitability to mean-revert. It overreacts to contemporary records of success and failure on the part of firms. It tends to project success to continue for prolonged periods into the future, overpricing successful firms. It also overestimates the length of time it will take unsuccessful firms to recover. The unsuccessful firms tend to sell at bargain prices.

The cheaper the stock, the better the outlook for future returns.

The positive payoff to a firm's rate of return on its book equity capital and total assets indicate that there is a significant degree of *imprecision* in the market's pricing. If the market assigns similar prices to firms with markedly different profitability, then other things—including price—being equal, the outlook for future return improves with more profitable companies in the portfolio.

Finally, two factors related to liquidity make the top twelve. First, we have annual trading volume (price-per-share times number of shares traded) as a percent of total market capitalization (price-per-share times the number of shares outstanding). This measures the degree of trading activity in the stock or the number of times the market capitalization turns over within a single year. As expected, the payoff to this measure of liquidity is negative—liquid stocks appear to have lower expected rates of return. The time trend in liquidity also appears as influential.

Where is risk?

Risk makes an appearance in the top twelve as the month-to-month variability in the ratio of cash flow-to-price ratio. Note that the greater this variability, the lower the expected return. Risk tends to be relatively important and perverted in its influence on expected return. This interesting tendency will be discussed at length later in the book.

Now look at the two middle panels of Table 4–1. Here we see the average payoffs in the *first and second* halves of the period.

Note that all the factors have the same sign for their average in the two halves as they did in the total. Even the magnitudes of the averages are remarkably similar.

We have also included in the table the mean payoffs as estimated in the period 1974 through 1999. The original study, published in the *Journal of Financial Economics,* ended in 1993. We see that the payoffs to technical history, cheapness, profitability, and risk continue unabated as they were originally reported in that study.

In Table 4–1 you are seeing the *true* determinants of expected stock returns.

Many finance professors find the stability and significance levels of these payoffs perplexing. That is because they are used to limiting the factors considered down to measures of *risk*. Most of the risk variables fail to make the top half, and their statistical significance pales in comparison.

Nevertheless, if the true determinants of stock returns are this stable over time, it would appear that our factor model would have a high degree of predictive power.

Let's see.

AFTERTHOUGHTS

The six families are not the end of the line.

Can you think of some additional factors that might be useful in predicting expected return? Some, for example, believe insider trading activity might be useful in this regard. Corporate insiders are required to report their trades to the S.E.C. This information is electronically available at a reasonable cost. Insider trading activity might be informative in two regards. First, in any given month, for a very small minority of stocks, insiders might be trading illegally on the basis of private information. For any given stock, this might constitute a strong signal, but over the broad cross-section of stocks it probably would not be picked up as a significant payoff in a factor model. However, directors and those in upper management routinely buy and sell shares from their personal holdings based on their overall opinions about the long-run prospects for the firm. Since this trading occurs over the broad cross-section of stocks, it might be more useful to a factor model in predicting expected return. However, you must distinguish between sales by insiders in this regard and purchases. Many sales of stock are motivated by the desire to reduce holdings for diversification purposes, as opposed to negative opinions regarding future prospects. Purchases are therefore more likely to be opinion-driven.

How would you design a factor that might be sensitive to illegal trading activity? Would it be based on the intensity of activity on the buy or sell side? How would you design a factor that would distinguish between routine insider purchases and sales?

Notes

1. See R. Haugen and N. Baker, "Commonality in the Determinants of Expected Stock Returns," *Journal of Financial Economics,* July 1996.

2. To determine the significance of the averages, we compute a measure of the extent to which they vary from month to month. This measure is called the standard error. The standard error is equal to the standard deviation of the monthly payoffs divided by the square root of the number of months over which the average is taken. By comparing the average to its standard error, one can determine the probability that the true expected value for the payoff is actually different from zero.

5

PREDICTING FUTURE STOCK RETURNS WITH THE EXPECTED-RETURN FACTOR MODEL

HOW WE ESTIMATE EXPECTED RETURN

Please go back and take another look at Table 3–3.

This is an example of the spreadsheet used to compute the relative expected rate of return to a single stock. Relative, because the bottom-line number is the difference between the particular stock's rate of return and the expected return to an average stock.

As indicated in Table 3–3, for each of the factors in the model, you multiply the stock's factor exposure by the projected payoff to the factor. This gives you the component of total expected return coming from the particular factor:

$$\text{Factor Exposure} \times \text{Projected Factor Payoff} =$$
$$\text{Factor Component of Exposure Return}$$

After doing this for each factor, you add up all the components to get the total relative expected return for the stock.

To test the predictive accuracy of our factor model, compute for all months, beginning with January 1979 and ending with December 1999, the expected return for each of the roughly 3,500 largest stocks in the U.S. population.[1] Factor exposures are based on information that would presumably have been available at the beginning of the month.[2] The projected factor payoffs are the simple moving averages of the trailing 12 estimated monthly payoffs.

HOW WE DID

Going into each month, we rank stocks by our estimates of total relative expected return. The 3,500 stocks are formed into (equally weighted) deciles of 350 stocks each. At the end of the month, we observe the returns actually produced. At the end of the month, we also update the estimates of expected return and reform the deciles for the next month. This completes the monthly cycle. At the end of each year, we compute the cumulative monthly realized rates of return over each year. Table 5–1 shows the accuracy of our predictions.

Decile 1 is the lowest expected-return decile. Decile 10 is highest. The ten numbers under the deciles are the realized rates of return by year and then across all the years.

Let's graph the results across all the years. Figure 5–1 plots the realized rates of return on the vertical axis against the decile numbers on the horizontal axis. The line of best fit going through the plot points has a slope of 3.2%. This is the expected increase in realized rates of return in going from one decile to the next. To get the spread in realized return between one end of the line and the other, you multiply the slope by 10 to get 32%.

32%!!

Not bad, I'd say.

To see the slopes for the other years, look at the second-to-last column of Table 5–1.

Note that the slopes are positive in *every year.*

The model is consistent from year to year because it employs so many factors. Growth stocks and value stocks tend to move in and out of favor. Over long periods, value tends to outperform, but when value is out of favor, growth tends to do well. The expected-return factor model does well in every year because its predictions are based partly on measures of cheapness (value) and partly on measures of profitability (growth).

A comprehensive list of factors brings predictive stability and predictive power.

The numbers in the last column of Table 5–1 show the fraction of the differences between the returns to the deciles explained by decile ranking. Note how large these numbers are. In several years, the fraction approaches 100%.

In Figure 5–2, we cumulate the rates of return and plot them on a log scale. Note how quickly the deciles order themselves in their relative performance.

Recall that in Chapter 3 we compared the predictive power of risk-factor models with naïve estimates of portfolio risk made over a trailing 60-month period. With the naïve estimates, we compute what the variance of the portfolio would have been in some past period and project that into the future. Risk-factor models *do* provide more accurate estimates than the naïve estimates, but the difference isn't profound.

Expected-return factor models may be another matter entirely. For expected return, the analogue to the naïve risk estimate is to calculate the average return to the portfolio over the past period and project *that* forward.

How would the accuracy of the naïve projection compare with the accuracy of the expected-return factor model?

Table 5–1 U.S. Realized Deciles Formed by Ranking on Expected Return

Deciles	1	2	3	4	5
Annual return					
1979	33.5%	32.6%	33.9%	43.1%	35.2%
1980	17.4	26.2	25.4	27.2	25.8
1981	−15.6	−14.2	−7.9	−4.6	2.1
1982	3.2	15.5	21.8	24.6	24.0
1983	11.8	18.0	23.4	29.5	28.8
1984	−30.9	−20.7	−13.4	−9.1	−6.5
1985	4.3	18.4	26.6	37.8	34.9
1986	−15.2	−7.1	1.9	9.2	12.1
1987	−23.8	−12.3	−5.0	−6.8	0.0
1988	1.5	10.4	18.5	24.0	22.2
1989	−3.0	8.2	9.7	16.8	18.7
1990	−46.9	−36.2	−27.5	−21.7	−15.5
1991	23.9	29.3	36.5	42.0	45.2
1992	2.5	7.5	16.3	20.3	17.8
1993	6.4	9.2	18.2	18.5	19.9
1994	−15.51	−8.20	−7.28	−4.10	−1.2
1995	15.01	15.10	29.34	28.34	26.1
1996	5.96	25.07	22.80	21.74	20.6
1997	8.75	23.32	23.38	27.06	32.7
1998	−26.73	−12.68	−7.49	−8.81	−10.0
1999	22.31	−0.73	0.27	4.64	4.5
Overall	−1.45%	5.37%	9.57%	12.42%	13.7%

Source: Reprinted from *Journal of Financial Economics,* 41, Robert Haugen and Nardin Baker, "Commonality in the Determinents of Expected Stock Returns," p. 414, Copyright 1996, with permission from Elsevier Science.

FIGURE 5–1 Expected Return Factor Model Decile Scatter Plot 1980-1999

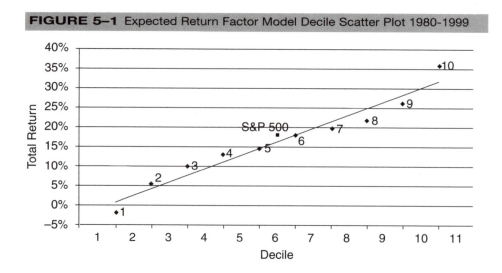

Table 5–1 *continued*

6	7	8	9	10	Slope	R-Squared
36.3%	47.3%	40.1%	39.3%	43.4%	1.1%	0.446
41.3	42.6	45.3	55.6	68.4	5.0	0.897
5.6	0.4	6.3	9.7	16.2	3.3	0.931
25.9	32.1	34.6	39.5	49.7	4.1	0.929
39.3	37.8	46.1	45.1	54.5	4.4	0.962
1.0	2.8	12.8	15.4	22.4	5.5	0.986
37.8	34.9	41.2	43.4	45.7	3.7	0.776
15.1	19.9	23.2	23.0	30.9	4.7	0.925
1.6	–3.4	–2.0	1.2	–5.1	1.8	0.486
28.8	26.9	25.9	29.7	27.0	2.5	0.714
21.5	28.5	29.8	32.4	28.7	3.6	0.893
–12.7	–10.2	–9.9	–2.9	1.3	4.8	0.937
45.7	51.1	46.6	46.9	57.4	3.1	0.817
15.7	17.1	18.9	21.1	24.5	1.8	0.619
20.1	20.0	20.7	24.2	22.2	1.6	0.738
22.3	21.6	24.0	27.1	30.9	3.5	0.932
–2.14	–0.24	8.96	7.28	10.01	2.6	0.931
37.56	31.99	33.58	42.15	53.55	3.5	0.832
24.85	17.30	21.91	15.93	25.47	0.6	0.093
26.74	35.91	37.95	45.15	51.75	3.8	0.899
1.09	–4.26	2.06	6.86	11.57	3.4	0.862
15.40	15.99	10.56	17.83	29.31	1.7	0.288
17.27%	18.56%	20.61%	24.69%	33.62%	3.2%	0.950%

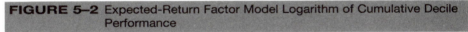

FIGURE 5–2 Expected-Return Factor Model Logarithm of Cumulative Decile Performance

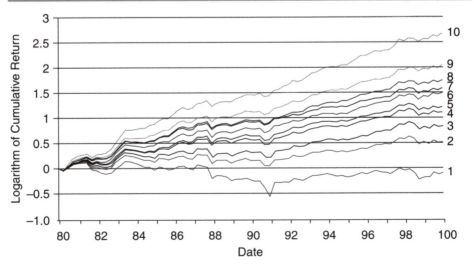

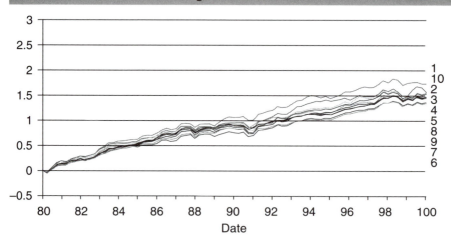

FIGURE 5–3 Naïve Model Logarithm of Cumulative Decile Performance

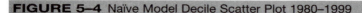

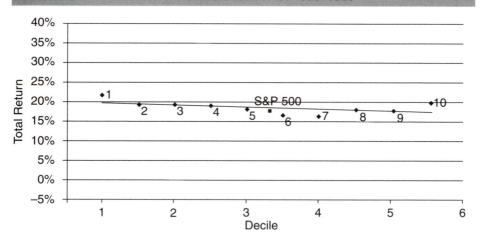

FIGURE 5–4 Naïve Model Decile Scatter Plot 1980–1999

To find out, we project forward, as the expected return for the next month, the average return for each of the 3,500 stocks over the trailing 60 months. Once again we form deciles based on the naïve projections.

The results of the experiment are presented in Figure 5–3. Note that the naïve models are actually perverted in terms of their predictions. The deciles predicted to do relatively well actually tended to *underperform*. A performance scatter plot is provided in Figure 5–4.

Remarkably, in spite of the relative strength of *expected-return* factor models, it is the *risk* models that have gained great popularity among practitioners and captured the attention of academics.

THE PROBLEM OF TURNOVER AND TRADING COSTS

Unfortunately, you can get the returns of decile 10 only if you can trade for *free*. Remember, the deciles are re-formed every month, and the expected returns projected by the factor model have a tendency to mean-revert. Moreover, this tendency is strongest in the extreme deciles 1 and 10.

Consequently, a great many of the stocks in these deciles will be leaving each month, probably to be replaced by stocks from deciles 2 through 9.

To see what fraction of the performance spread is "eaten" by trading costs, we will simulate the performance of a trading strategy in which we employ the Markowitz optimization tool to find portfolios in the efficient set.

We're going to make several changes in methodology, all of which will serve to narrow the spreads of Table 5–1.

First, we shift from the Russell 3000 stock population to the Russell 1000—roughly the 1,000 largest stocks in the U.S. market. These are the focus of institutional investors, and it will be interesting to gauge the predictive power of the model in the big stocks. *Second,* we move from monthly to quarterly rebalancing. *Third,* we will control portfolio turnover. *Fourth,* we will account for the cost of trading. We will assume a 2% total cost associated with the roundtrip of buying and selling. This is as much as ten times the actual cost of trading in stocks this large. *Finally,* these results will be restricted to the 1979-93 period covered in our original paper.

We will attempt to build portfolios on an efficient set similar to that of Figure 2–1A.

The constraints imposed in finding the portfolios are stated in Exhibit 5–1. These constraints are merely designed to limit the "bets"[3] we take in individual stocks and industries. The constraints prevent the optimization process from "plunging" or over-investing in particular stocks or industries. The results of the test aren't very sensitive to reasonable modifications in these constraints.

First, we will attempt to go for the nose of the efficient set—the stock portfolio with the lowest possible risk *period*. We'll use a naïve approach in finding this portfolio. At the beginning of each quarter, we look back to the preceding 24 months, and we find the portfolio with the lowest trailing volatility of return.[4] We hold this portfolio for one quarter, and then rebalance into the new portfolio with trailing 24-month volatility. This continues for the total period 1979 to 1993. Call this portfolio *G*.

Next, we try to build a portfolio with a higher expected return. We are armed, from the factor model, with estimates of expected return for each stock. At the beginning of each quarter, we try to build (with Harry's portfolio optimization tool) a portfolio with a level of risk between *G* and the risk of the Russell 1000 Index. We hold the portfolio for a quarter, and then we rebalance under the same objective, at the beginning of the next quarter. Call this portfolio *I*.

Now we go for a portfolio with even higher return. Our objective is to aim for the risk level of the Index. Call this portfolio *H*.[5]

<table>
<tr><td colspan="2" align="center">**EXHIBIT 5–1**</td></tr>
<tr><td colspan="2" align="center">**OPTIMIZATION CONSTRAINTS**</td></tr>
</table>

1. The maximum weight in a portfolio that can be assigned to a single stock is limited to 5%. The minimum is 0%. (Short selling is not permitted.)

2. No more than three times its percentage of the Russell 1000 total market capitalization can be invested in any one stock in the portfolio.

3. The portfolio industry weight is restricted to within 3% of the market capitalization weight of that industry.[6]

4. Turnover in the portfolio is constrained from 20% to 40% annually, depending on the emphasis in the optimization toward higher expected return.

Finally, we turn Harry's tool in reverse and try to build a portfolio with a low expected return. This portfolio is constructed under the same constraints as the first three. The level of aggressiveness in pursuing low expected return is approximately the same as *H* in its pursuit of high return. Call this one *L*.

The performance of these four portfolios relative to the Russell 1000 Index is presented in Figure 5–5.

Note that the *G* portfolio actually outperforms the index. Recall that *G* was dedicated only to risk minimization. Its outperformance is further evidence that the payoff to risk is *negative* during the period of the test.

As anticipated, climbing the efficient set with the factor model produces additional returns. Portfolio *I*, which emphasizes low risk over high return, outperforms by more than the *G* portfolio. In aiming for market-level risk, the *H* portfolio, which turns out to actually have similar volatility to the market, outperforms the market by nearly 4% (400 basis points).

Portfolio turnover increases, as attempts to capture extra return become more aggressive. Turnover runs from as low as 20% per year for Portfolio *G* to 40% per year for *H*.

The *L* portfolio lies to the southeast. In building *L*, we were looking for stocks with low expected return. The optimizer that built *L* emphasized low return over minimizing risk.

It didn't do a very good job at minimizing risk, did it?

Why?

Because in building L, the optimizer searched for stocks with low expected return. Peculiar as it may seem, these stocks, as well as the portfolios built with them, tend to have *high* volatility. The relationship between risk and return is upside down within the stock market.

In terms of its realized return, the highly volatile *L* portfolio underperforms *H*, its high-return counterpart, by approximately 9%.

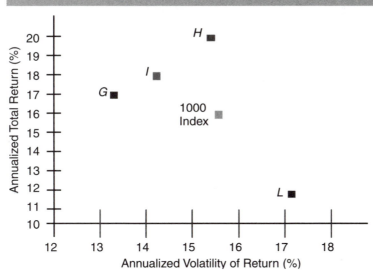

FIGURE 5–5 Optimized Portfolios in the Russell 1000 Population: 1979 to 1993

Even though *L* is more volatile, an efficient-markets professor would likely argue that, for some reason, *H* is the more risky of the two, and the difference in their returns is really a risk premium.

For example, Fama and French (F&F)[7] might claim that the 900 basis-point differential is really a risk premium that was expected to be received by investors all along. When they see such differentials, they like to "risk-adjust" them.

They have chosen to believe that the risk of a stock is accounted for by three factors:

- The monthly difference between the return to the market and the risk-free rate (*market*)
- The monthly difference between the return to small stocks and large stocks (*size*)[8]
- The monthly difference between the return to value stocks and growth stocks (*value/growth*)[9]

F&F also use a multiple-regression approach. With our factor model, we try to explain why different stocks have different returns *within a single month*. F&F, on the other hand, try to explain why a single portfolio of stocks has different returns *from month to month*.

What they do is similar to what we discussed under the Arbitrage Pricing Theory. With APT, the factors are usually numbers from the macro-economy. F&F have chosen to risk-adjust returns by taking numbers mostly from the stock market. With APT, you obtain things like inflation beta—the sensitivity of stock return to inflation. F&F also obtain betas, but these tell of the portfolio's sensitivity to things like the relative performance of value and growth stocks.

As a result of their process, F&F obtain an estimate[10] of the portfolio's expected return in a market environment where:

- The market produces a return equal to Treasury bills
- The performance of small and large stocks is the same
- The performance of value and growth stocks is the same

F&F firmly believe that this estimate provides a very good measure of risk-adjusted performance.[11]

Let's use their procedure to risk-adjust the returns to portfolio H and L:

Risk-adjusted Annualized Return: $H = 5.03\%$; $L = -7.44\%$

Risk adjustment actually widens the spread from 900 to 1,247 basis points.

The return reduction for risk is actually much bigger for L than it is for H.

This must mean that, by F&F's own measure, the risk of L is greater than that of H.

Getting interesting?[12]

AFTERTHOUGHTS

Interestingly, the predictive power of the factor model improves as you move from groups of large companies to groups of small companies. That is, decile slopes, such as those presented in Table 5–1, are decidedly greater for a small stock population like the Russell 2000 than they are for a large stock population such as the S&P 500. Why might we expect this to be the case? Large stocks can be thought of as portfolios of individual enterprises. As such, the individual characteristics, which collectively represent their profiles, will be blended across the components. In contrast, small stocks are likely to be more individualistic and heterogeneous with respect to their nature. If their profiles are more heterogeneous, their expected returns, as predicted by the model, will be as well. That is, the spread in expected return between decile 1 and 10 will be larger if the deciles are constructed over small stocks than they will be if they are constructed over large ones. As might be expected, the spread in the realized returns, and the slopes, turn out to be larger as well.

Notes

1. Prior to 1993, the population roughly consisted of the Russell 3000 stock population. After 1993 it roughly consisted of the largest 3500 U. S. stocks, where required data was available.

2. Prior to 1988, we assume a three-month reporting lag. During and after 1988, we use the actual data files that would have been available to someone trying to use the model.

3. Over- or under-weighting relative to the weights in the Russell 1000 Index.

4. Even though there are 24 months and 1,000 stocks, given our constraints, there is a unique solution to the problem. We find that solution through a numerical search procedure. Thus, we need not invert the covariance matrix.

5. Here and elsewhere, I have argued for a negative payoff to risk. One might ask, "If the relationship between risk and return is negative, how can there be a positively sloped efficient set?" If we plot expected return vertically and risk horizontally, think of an egg-shaped plot of the positions of individual stocks. The egg is tilted to the northwest, reflecting the negative payoff to risk. The egg still has an efficient set (albeit a small one) running from near the most westerly position of the egg to near the most northerly.

6. Based on the two-digit SIC code.

7. See E. Fama and K. French, "Multifactor Explanations of Asset Pricing Anomalies," *Journal of Finance,* March 1996, pp. 55–84.

8. In our tests, *size* is found by monthly ranking the stocks in the Russell 3000 by total market capitalization (market price times number of shares). Equally weighting the returns to the largest 20% gives us the return to large stocks. Doing the same for the bottom 20% gives the return to small stocks.

9. The 3,000 stocks are ranked monthly on the book-to-price ratio. Equally weighting the returns to the highest 20% gives the return to value stocks and weighting to the lowest 20%, the return to growth stocks.

10. The estimate is the constant term for a regression in which the dependent variable is the portfolio's return, and the independent variables are *market, size,* and *value/growth.*

11. I have no idea why they believe this to be true.

12. In a recent University of Chicago working paper, "Profitability in the Cross-section of Stock Returns" by J. Douglass Hanna and Mark Ready, the authors successfully replicate the results of the Haugen and Baker study. They examine the results of trading strategies that go long in decile 10 and short in decile 1. They find that, assuming a one-day delay between model estimation and trading, the net results of a highly active strategy of holding only decile 1 stocks during each month and shorting only decile 1 stocks each month indicates a positive but insignificant performance after trading costs. A less active strategy whereby the stocks held long are held until they fall below decile 7 results in a positive and highly significant net performance after trading costs. However, in practice, one would be foolish in following either of these strategies. Rather, it is best to employ the expected returns in conjunction with a risk model in a process of portfolio optimization and rebalancing. As discussed in this chapter, we employed such a process in our original tests and concluded that the net results were economically significant even after allowing for trading costs that were, in general, *higher* than those assumed by Hanna and Ready. It is also the case that actual users of the model estimate after the close of trading on a given day and then trade at the open of the next day. Thus, we do not see the rationale for their one-day delay.

6

COUNTERATTACK—THE FIRST WAVE

When they're not screaming *"Risk premium!"* the professors from the College of Cardinals like to cry *"Bias!"*

You see, results inconsistent with their religion *must* be biased.

So if you're going to offer evidence against what's taught in the catechism, you had better be prepared for a series of ferocious attacks.

We're prepared for battle.

SURVIVAL BIAS

The ground under our feet shakes. Here comes the first wave of cavalry thundering over the hill, and, by George, they're screaming *"Survival Bias!"*

What's that?

Survival Bias occurs if individual firms that go inactive during the test period are systematically excluded from the test population.

Consider studies of the performance of mutual funds, for example.

Suppose all mutual funds have *identical expected rates of return* (equal to that of the market), but different volatilities, as in the probability distributions of Figure 6–1. Assume also that, if performance falls below the threshold indicated in the figure, they go out of business. Then the probability of reaching that threshold *increases* with the *risk* of the fund.

If we observe the performance of only those funds that remain active, we will tend to find that the average performance of the surviving funds exceeds that of the market. To see why, consider Figure 6–2 on page 62. Each point in the figure represents one of our hypothetical mutual funds. We plot realized return on the vertical scale, and monthly volatility on the horizontal. Note that the range of possible outcomes is wider for the more risky funds.

We will also tend to find that performance increases with the level of variability in return, as with the x's of Figure 6–2. The o's in the figure represent the funds that fell below the threshold, didn't survive, and were not included in the test. The line drawn through the scatter of x's is the line of best fit. It has a positive slope.

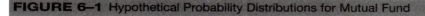

FIGURE 6–1 Hypothetical Probability Distributions for Mutual Fund

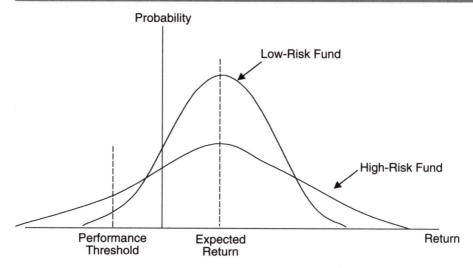

Thus, it will appear to us that we can predict performance on the basis of fund risk. We detect a positive payoff to risk and we predict that the more risky the fund, the higher its expected return.[1]

In the case of our model, if the factors used in prediction are somehow related to the probability of going inactive, failure to include inactive firms in the database will result in misleading estimates of predictive power.[2]

Does our test suffer from Survival Bias?

No.

In the original 1996 study, our population of firms included the firms that were actually in the Russell 1000 and 2000 Stock Indexes at the beginning of each quarter.[3] We weren't able to find all the firms that were ever in the index, but after years of searching we came pretty close.

In addition, given the nature of our results described in the next chapter, Survival Bias, even if it were present, would work against us rather than in our favor. We find that the stocks with the highest return are bigger and more profitable. One can hardly argue that this is the product of Survival Bias.

Sorry. No Survival Bias here.

LOOK-AHEAD BIAS

And now, from the direction of our left flank, spitfire, black smoke, and the crack of rifle shots. The Temple's ground infantry is shouting, "*Look-Ahead Bias!*"

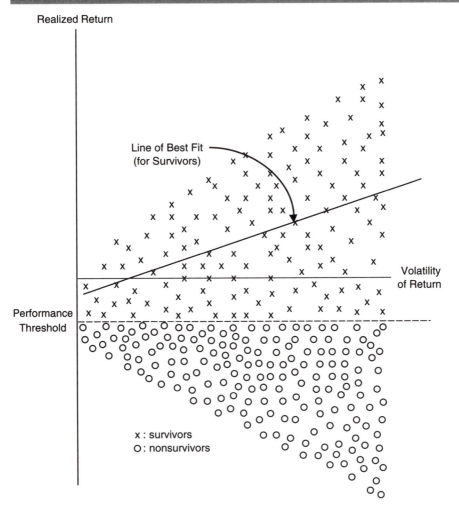

FIGURE 6–2 Hypothetical Distribution of Outcomes for Mutual Funds

Look-Ahead Bias occurs when you calculate factor exposures using data items that wouldn't have been known when the predictions were made.

Please refer back to Table 3–3. Suppose you are forecasting expected returns for March 1988. Your forecasts are the product of projected factor payoffs and contemporary factor exposures. The question is, "Did you use information that wasn't released until after February 28th to compute the exposures?"

If you did, you're *cheating*. We'd all like to know information before it's announced, wouldn't we?

Here's an example of how Look-Ahead Bias can mislead us.

Suppose that the earnings-to-price ratio is used as a predictive factor. If the ratio is calculated with an earnings number that was unreported as of the date of prediction, the factor's predictive power will be exaggerated. This is because the set of firms with relatively high-earnings yields will include those with *unexpectedly high (but unreported)* earnings for the fourth quarter. Market reactions to these numbers are likely to be positive. Thus, high earnings-to-price ratios will be associated with high subsequent returns, even though there may be no *true* predictive information in the number whatsoever.

Does our test suffer from Look-Ahead Bias?

Not likely.

For the period prior to 1987, we assumed a three-month lag between the end of each quarter and the reporting of the accounting numbers. If that's not long enough to satisfy the Cardinals, after 1987 we began saving our files. After 1987, we used the actual files that would have been available to an analyst at the time the exposures were calculated.

If you look back at Table 5–1, there's not much of a difference in the results before and after 1987.

No Look-Ahead Bias here.

BID-ASKED BOUNCE

What now? A blast of artillery from the ridge over our *right* flank. As the cannonballs hit the ground around us, they seem to do the *Bid-Asked Bounce.*

Bid-Asked Bounce?

Another insidious bias.

Stocks trade at bid or asked prices, depending on whether the trade was a buy or a sell. Returns are measured close-to-close, irrespective of whether the closing price was at the bid or the asked price.

Suppose that the underlying market value of a stock does not change during months 1 and 2 of Figure 6–3. As you can see, the last trade of month 1 was at the bid. There is roughly an even chance that the stock traded at the asked price at the *beginning* of month 1 and at the end of month 2.

This being the case, the measured return will either be zero or negative for the first month and either zero or positive for the next.

Therefore, we may seem to observe short-term reversal patterns in stock returns, even when there are none. Thus, the existence of Bid-Asked Bounce can lead a researcher to falsely conclude that last month's return has predictive power, even when it is completely unrelated to the next month's return.

Are our results a product of the Bid-Asked Bounce?

Assuredly not.

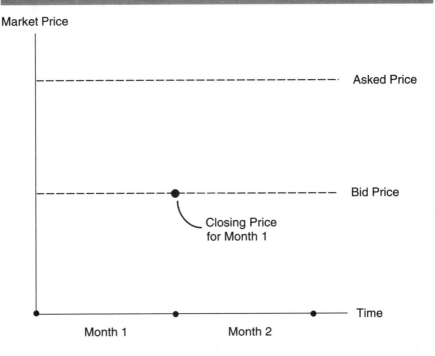

FIGURE 6–3 An Illustration of Bid-Asked Bounce

To determine the extent to which Bid-Asked Bounce influences our results, we leave a month out between the time the expected returns are calculated and the time the trades are to be made.

It's as though we make our calculations and then go on a month's vacation before we bother to trade.

The effect of this is to slightly reduce the slopes of Figure 5–1 and slightly increase the percentages of the differences in decile realized returns we are able to explain by decile ranking (the R-squares).

Sorry, but the Bounce is not on us.

DATA SNOOPING

And now, on horseback, atop the hill to our rear, five men peer at us through powerful binoculars. They are the scouts of the Army of Modern Finance. They carry a flag. It bears the fearsome words "*Data Snooping.*"

A Data Snooper reads papers written by others that report that unusual stock returns seem to be associated with things like short-[4], intermediate-[5], and long-term[6] past returns, book-to-price ratios,[7] earnings-to-price ratios,[8] and measures of liquidity.[9] These papers give them good ideas about factors that should be included in an expected-return model. *Then they test their model using the same data as the other studies.*

Not fair.

I would now like to stand and humbly confess to being a Data Snooper. I did read the papers. So what can I say?

Three things.

First, all the studies that I read before doing the original tests ended, at the latest, in the year 1990. In spite of this, our results still persist through 1999. Second, in Chapter 8, we take the model international and find similar results in countries that haven't been snooped. Finally, I will shortly show you results for a real portfolio, constructed with the expected-return factor model, that couldn't *possibly* be the result of snooping.

DATA MINING

Now, from our left rear, a brigade of coal-dirty men wearing yellow helmets adorned with little lanterns charges down toward us. Their banner bears the *fighting* words "*Data Mining.*"

Data Mining is an inflammatory charge.

A Data Miner spins the computer thousands of times. Tries a thousand ways to beat the market.

You'll always find one way in a thousand.

That's the one that looks interesting. That's the one you publish.

Unethical, Data Mining is.

Problem with Data Mining, however, is that the "lucky" list of factors is bound to look pretty *fluky*.

On the other hand, our list looks very *basic*.

That's because it's the *first* list we tried.

COUNTERFEIT

But, good Lord! Look who followed the miners over the hill. It's the Temple Choir, marching and singing "It's Only a *Paper* Moon."

What kind of a battlefield is this, anyway?

The rest of the first bar goes, "Sure you can beat the market on *paper,* but just try it for *real.*"

True, there's a big difference between paper money and real money, but, fortunately, we can prove that this factor model works "on the front lines."

On December 16th 1996, *Business Week* published an article about the expected-return factor model discussed in this book. The article featured an investment management firm called Analytic Investors, which was among the first to adopt the technology. Analytic continues to use the technology to this date. They use the expected-return model in conjunction with a risk factor model to manage a neutral, core investment strategy in which there is no tilt toward either value or growth. Analytic restricts their stock population to those included in the S&P 500 stock index, and they rebalance their positions on a monthly basis. They began their strategy in 1996 and currently manage more than $1 billion in the core composite. Since then, they have been steadfast in their implementation.

Figure 6–4 shows their AMIR compliant performance across their composite. Annualized average return is plotted vertically and annualized monthly standard deviation of return is plotted horizontally. The time period covered extends from October 1996 through December 2000. The S&P 500 is also plotted in the graph. Note that Analytic has approximately the same risk with an annualized average premium in their return of 4.30%.

The results presented in this book are *not* based on Survival Bias, Look-Ahead Bias, Bid-Asked Bounce, Data Snooping, or Data Mining.

They are *real*.

AFTERTHOUGHTS

For the past few years I have provided monthly estimates of expected return, based on a factor model similar in form to the one discussed in this book, to a wide variety of institutional investors, including pension funds, endowments, and professional money managers. Based on electronic feeds of information about corporate accounting data, macroeconomic numbers, and stock returns, factor values are computed, based on the closing prices on the last day of the month. Within hours, the payoffs to each factor are computed, and, based on the trailing history of these payoffs, the payoffs for the next month are projected forward. Expected returns for the month are then computed and electronically mailed to each client. Clients then use optimizers to rebalance their portfolios at the open on the next trading day.

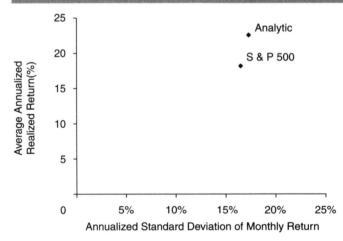

FIGURE 6–4 The Performance of Analytic Investors Composite Portfolio

We have developed a history of the numbers mailed to clients that are subject to audit. These numbers are obviously completely free of any of the biases discussed in this chapter. Stocks are ranked by our predictions and formed into deciles. The realized returns to the deciles are presented in the following table. The returns for 2000 are through August.

Decile	1	2	3	4	5	6	7	8	9	10
1997	9.6%	19.7%	20.1%	19.7%	32.8%	32.15%	37.3%	39.2%	52.5%	61.55%
1998	-27.0%	-11.7%	-11.4%	-5.3%	-1.6%	-1.7%	1.0%	3.6%	8.2%	7.6%
1999	12.5%	9.5%	5.0%	6.8%	10.2%	12.4%	11.3%	18.0%	34.9%	40.6%
2000	-5.8%	3.0%	4.2%	7.3%	13.4%	14.5%	17.8%	21.4%	32.4%	36.6%

These results are not back-tests, and the predictive power of the factor model speaks for itself.

Notes

1. For studies of portfolios of individual firms, the nature of the bias is less clear because many firms can disappear because of merger as well as failure. In either case, it is likely that the overall returns to nonsurvivors will be abnormal.

2. Survival Bias is exacerbated by the nature of firms that tend to be back-filled in commercial databases. Providers tend to add companies that have significant market positions when the records are back-filled. Thus, given two firms of identical size five years prior to the back-fill, the larger (and more successful) firm at the time of the back-fill is more likely to be added to the database.

3. We wish to thank the Frank Russell Company for providing us with a history of the list.

4. See N. Jegadeesh, "Evidence of Predictable Behavior of Security Returns," *Journal of Finance,* 1990.

5. See N. Jegadeesh and S. Titman, "Returns to Buying Winners and Selling Losers," *Journal of Finance,* 1993.

6. See W. DeBondt and R. Thaler, "Does the Stock Market Overreact?" *Journal of Finance,* 1985.

7. See E. Fama and K. French, "The Cross-section of Expected Stock Returns," *Journal of Finance,* 1992.

8. See S. Basu, "Investment Performance of Common Stocks in Relation to Their Price-earnings Ratios—A Test of the Efficient Market Hypothesis," *Journal of Finance,* June 1977.

9. Y. Amihud and H. Mendelson, "Asset Pricing and the Bid-Ask Spread," *Journal of Financial Economics,* 1986.

10. Therefore, they are always *fully* invested in Japan.

7

SUPER STOCKS AND
STUPID STOCKS

Now that the dust of battle has settled, a lingering question remains.

Are the differential returns of Table 5–1 *somehow* related to risk differentials between the deciles?

This is a difficult question. The researchers of Modern Finance seem to be labeling *any* premium they see in realized returns a *risk* premium. With the asset pricing theories of Modern Finance in a state of discredit and disarray, how is one to distinguish the *expected* from the *surprise?*

In the past, tests of market efficiency were considered joint tests. That is, you had to first assume the validity of a particular asset-pricing model. This assumption gave you an estimate of the return an efficient market would be expecting from a portfolio. Then you compared this estimate with the portfolio's realized returns to see if the two returns were inconsistent with the efficient market.

Fortunately, given the nature of the results presented on the following pages, we don't need strong assumptions about the nature of stock pricing in an efficient market.

We need only one assumption.

Investors don't like risk.

RISK IN THE RETURNS

We begin our investigation by examining the distributions of decile returns.

As discussed in Chapter 2, investors have demonstrated a clear preference for *positive* skewness in the distribution of returns to their investments. Perhaps the returns distribution shifts from skewed right to skewed left as we move from decile 1 to decile 10.

Figure 7–1 provides the answer to this question. It shows the frequency distribution of monthly returns to the extreme deciles over the period 1980 through 1999, decile 1 as represented by the shaded bars and decile 10 by the white bars.

FIGURE 7–1 Frequency Distribution of Monthly Return for Deciles 1 and 10

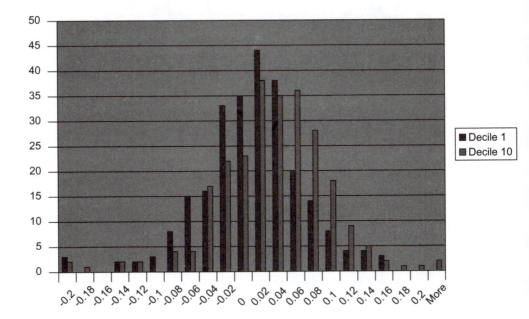

Both distributions show some evidence of negative skewness. However, if anything, the distribution for decile 1 looks worse in this respect than the distribution for decile 10.

It would be difficult to make a case that the extremely high returns to decile 10 stem from a relatively scary distribution of returns.

But maybe it's the way the returns relate to other stocks that's scary.

Maybe we can find the answer with the risk-adjustment model of Fama and French.

Recall that F&F risk-adjust by relating a portfolio's monthly returns to three factors—market, size, and value/growth.

In the process they obtain three betas, or sensitivities, for the portfolio:

- Sensitivity to market returns
- Sensitivity to the relative performance of small and large stocks
- Sensitivity to the relative performance of value and growth stocks.

In allowing for the sensitivity of the portfolio's returns to each of the three factors, F&F asked the following question, "What would we expect the portfolio's return to be in a market environment where: (1) There was no risk premium (beyond the T bill return for the S&P 500, (2) Small and large stocks produced the same returns, and (3) Neither value nor growth

Table 7–1 Decile Risk-Adjusted Annualized Returns, 1980 to 1999	
Decile	*Risk-Adjusted Return*
1	−00.33%
2	4.75
3	7.27
4	8.61
5	10.99
6	12.87
7	14.10
8	17.73
9	20.02
10	27.39

out-performed." This statistical expectation becomes F&F's risk-adjusted return.

What about F&F's risk-adjusted measures of return for the 10 deciles in the period 1980–99?

They look like what you see in Table 7–1.

It seems safe to conclude that, the return differentials in the deciles is not cased by the F&F risk factors.

RISK IN THE CORPORATE PROFILE

Risk is multifaceted.

An ugly balance sheet may not show up in the volatility of returns because it remains *unchangingly* ugly in every month. In the face of its unfortunate but stable condition, the stock price *is* depressed. But it *remains* depressed.

Stock volatility feeds on *change*.

Perhaps there is something about the more permanent profile of decile 10 that gives investors cause for serious concern.

To determine if this is true, we will, across the period of 1989–99 and across all firms in the deciles, average the exposures to each factor to compute a corporate profile for each of the deciles. The profiles are presented in Figures 7–2 through 7–7.

Figure 7–2 profiles the *risk* characteristics of the deciles. In terms of market risk, the table shows the average beta (ranging from 1.12 for decile 1 to .97 for decile 10) and average volatility of the stocks in each decile.

Consistent with the results of the previous section, the risk associated with market returns falls as we move from decile 1 through decile 10.

Also shown on the graph are the average debt-to-equity ratios and the number of times, on average, each firm covered its interest charges

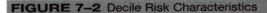

FIGURE 7–2 Decile Risk Characteristics

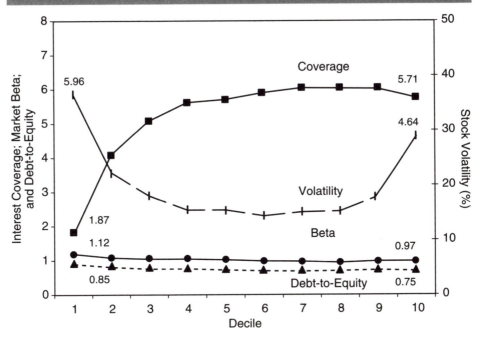

with operating income. In going from decile 1 to decile 10, the firms have progressively less debt, and interest charges become smaller and smaller relative to operating income. In short, the firms of decile 10 are in much better financial shape than the firms of decile 1.

Figure 7–3 profiles the size of the firms in the deciles and the liquidity of the stocks. As we go from left to right, the firms become larger and more liquid.[6] The market price per share is also larger. The performance of decile 10 cannot be attributed to the astronomical returns of a few penny stocks, shooting, at some point, from a price of a few pennies to a few dollars.

The technical history of the stock prices is profiled in Figure 7–4. While the lower deciles tend to have lower returns in the previous month. However, as we move from 2 to 12 months in the return, we see negative momentum relative to the market for the deciles on the left and positive momentum for those on the right.

Figures 7–5 and 7–6 profile profitability. Average levels of profitability are profiled in Figure 7–5. The left-hand deciles are clearly unprofitable in all dimensions. They are losing money now, and their earnings have been declining over the previous five years.

But as we move from left to right in Figure 7–5, there is significant improvement in *every* dimension. There are more sales relative to assets (asset turnover), much higher profit margins, and rates of return on assets

FIGURE 7–3 Size and Liquidity Characteristics

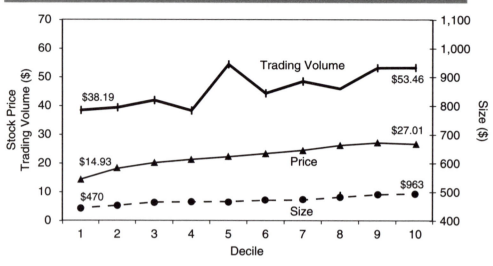

FIGURE 7–4 Technical History

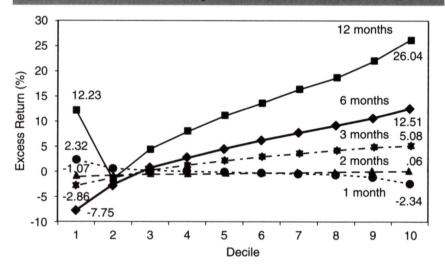

and equity that are also dramatically higher. Earnings per share are also growing faster in the trailing five-year period.

Moving to Figure 7–6, we see the trailing five-year trends in profitability. For the firms in the left deciles, we see a picture of *deterioration* through negative trends in asset turnover, profit margins, and return on assets and equity. Here, things are bad and in the process of getting worse.

On the other hand, as we move to the right, the trends turn from negative to positive.

FIGURE 7–5 Current Profitability

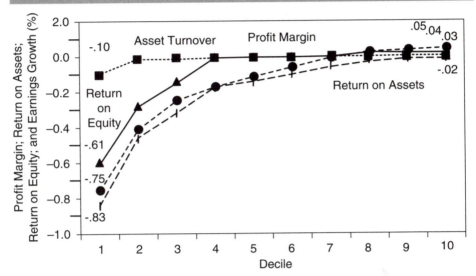

FIGURE 7–6 Profitability Trends (Growth In)

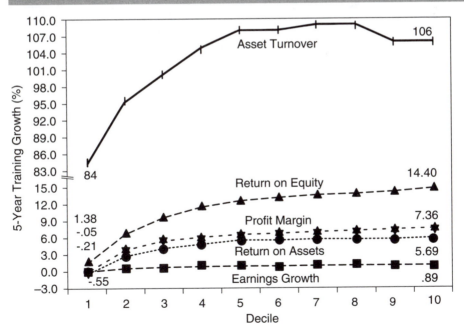

Good and getting *better.*

But portfolios this good must surely be expensive. Let's check it out.

Figure 7–7 presents the real surprise. Here we see the ratios of sales, cash flow, earnings, dividends, sales, and book-to-price.

FIGURE 7–7 Price Level

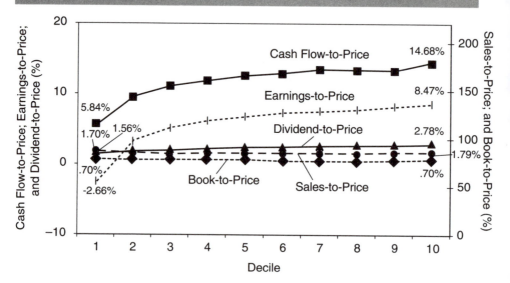

As incredible as it seems, the right-hand portfolios are actually selling very *cheap* in the market relative to cash flow, earnings, and dividends. The left-hand portfolios, as unattractive as they seem to be, are actually *expensive* in these terms.

Think of the decile 10 profile.

Imagine stocks that are big, liquid, financially sound, low-risk, momentum in the market, profitable in every dimension, and becoming more profitable in every way. *Yet they sell at dirt-cheap market prices.*

This is a *dream* profile, the profile of a stock you would love to own. We shall call this the profile of a *Super Stock.*

Let me ask you a question: Have you ever seen an individual stock that looks like that?

No?

That's because no single stock has the complete profile.

You see, Super Stocks go around disguised as mild-mannered securities. Each has one or more components of the profile, but not the whole thing. If a single stock "walked around" with the complete profile, even the inefficient market would price it up to where it was no longer selling cheap. It's only when Super Stocks are assembled into a portfolio (like decile 10) that they remove their eyeglasses and reveal their true identities.

And what about the profile of decile 1?

Disgustingly *ugly!*

These stocks are relatively small, illiquid, risky, financially shaky, have negative momentum, unprofitable now and getting worse, yet are selling at high prices relative to current sales, cash flow, and earnings.

Stupid Stocks.

Contrast Stupid Stocks with a cheap value stock. The earnings of a value stock may be going down. The market overreacts and the price falls further, and now the stock sells at a bargain price. In the case of Stupid Stocks, for the portfolio as a whole, the earnings are falling fast. Market prices in the portfolio do fall, but not as fast as earnings. Consequently, the portfolio sells at high cash flow, earnings, and dividend multiples in spite of its sordid condition. It's *expensive.*

Why does a market that generally overreacts to failure seem to underreact in this case? As with Super Stocks, there is no single Stupid Stock with the *complete* profile. So we're not seeing an underreaction to the misfortune befalling a single stock. The market doesn't underreact to a unique *event.*

Contrast a Super Stock portfolio with an expensive growth stock. In the case of the growth stock, the earnings are going up, and the market overreacts to success, driving the price of the stock up to the point where it becomes expensive—too expensive. In the case of a Super Stock portfolio, on average, the earnings are rising rapidly. The average price goes up too, but not as fast.[7] On average, the portfolio sells cheap in the market.

Again, how can an overreactive market underreact in this way? Here, too, since there is no single Super Stock, there is no unique *event* to which the market underreacts.

Look closely at Figures 7–2 through 7–7.

The inefficient market is speaking to us clearly and loudly.

These deciles were constructed *solely* on the basis of our estimates of expected return. There was no explicit attempt to form any particular profile within the deciles. The strikingly different profiles emerge naturally.

Listen to your intuition.

Doesn't it tell you that, if you *could* put together a portfolio with the spectacularly beautiful profile of a decile 10, it would produce superior returns in the future?

Doesn't it tell you that, if you *could* construct a portfolio as scary and ugly as that of decile 1, it would produce terrible returns in the future?

Well, you *can* and they *will.*

Your intuition is completely correct. *It* is more powerful than *all* the theories of Modern Finance.

What we didn't understand before was the ready availability of Stupid and Super Stock portfolios. Now we know they *are* available. And we have built them without even trying.

And wait until you see what we can build when we *try.*

AFTERTHOUGHTS

Think about how the profiles of the deciles would look if the stock market were truly efficient. In an efficient market, the stocks of decile 1, with its lowest expected future returns, would be characterized by low risk. The stocks in the lower deciles would have lower market risk—lower volatility of returns and lower market betas. They would have lower financial risk—less debt and higher interest coverage. They would be more liquid and less costly to trade. Investors in the efficient market would know this and price the stocks up accordingly, lowering their expected returns, placing them in the lower deciles. In an efficient market, we wouldn't necessarily see the more expensive stocks in the lower deciles, but what we certainly wouldn't expect to see is a pattern where the cheaper and the more expensive stocks are both in the upper deciles.

The patterns that we see in Figure 7–7 are, in nearly all respects, inconsistent with an efficient market.

Notes

1. Nine of the ten deciles carry market betas that are greater than one. This is because the deciles are equally weighted and the market index used to compute the betas is capitalization-weighted and, therefore, dominated by the largest stocks.

2. See R. Haugen, E. Talmor, and W. Torous, "The Effect of Volatility Changes on the Level of Stock Prices and Subsequent Expected Returns," *Journal of Finance,* 1991; and K. French, W. Schwert, and R. Stambaugh, "Expected Stock Return and Volatility," *Journal of Financial Economics,* 1987.

3. All the betas are statistically significantly different from zero at better than a 99% level of confidence.

4. All the betas are statistically significantly different from zero at better than 95% confidence except those for deciles 8 and 9.

5. See, for example, J. Lakonishok, A. Shleifer, and A. Vishny, "Contrarian Investment, Extrapolation, and Risk," *Journal of Finance,* 1994.

6. It may seem strange that the high-return deciles are more liquid, when we know that liquidity has a negative payoff. Actually, the powerful profitability family is greatly influencing the construction of the deciles. Liquidity and profitability are correlated. Liquidity merely "comes along for the ride."

7. This is why Super Stocks are not especially cheap relative to book values. Relative to cash flow and earnings, book values are stable numbers. Value stocks become cheap relative to book value because their *market prices* overreact to firm misfortune. It's the prices that move to make them cheap, not the book values. In the case of Super Stocks, it's the cash flows and earnings that move to make them cheap, not the prices.

8

THE INTERNATIONAL RESULTS

We have seen the power of the expected-return factor model in the United States. We now travel to four other countries—France, Germany, Japan, and the United Kingdom.

We shall employ the same menu of factors that was used in the United States. It's important to note that each country will be modeled separately. This is because, over the time period of these tests, the factor payoffs seem to be uncorrelated across international boundaries.

We use as our database Compustat's Global Vantage. Given that we need a trailing five-year period to compute earnings growth rates, trends, betas, and volatilities, the earliest starting point is 1985. As with the initial United States study, the international study concludes in 1993.

WHAT PAYS OFF ACROSS THE WORLD

Once again, we rank the factors based on average (across the five countries) statistical significance.[1] The 12 most important factors are presented in Table 8–1. In the first column under each country, we see the average payoff over the 108 months from 1985 through 1993. Next to the average, we see the statistical probability that the underlying expected value for the factor payoff is truly different from zero.

Perhaps the most striking feature of the table is that the signs for the payoffs are the same across all the countries! This is the case even though each country is modeled separately!

And all of our friends are back.

We see evidence of short-term reversal patterns in stock returns (negative payoffs on one- and three-month returns), intermediate-term momentum (positive payoffs to 12-month return), long-term reversals (negative payoffs on five-year return), cheapness paying off positively (positive payoffs on book-to-price, cash flow-to-price, earnings-to-price, and sales-to-price), and profitability paying off positively (positive payoffs on return on equity). Risk now makes the top-factors list big time. Unfortunately, all the payoffs have the same sign, and it is inconsistent with the predictions of Modern Finance. We see negative payoffs on the debt-to-equity ratio, variability of a stock's

Table 8–1 Mean Payoffs and Confidence Levels for the 12 Most Important Factors of the World, 1985 to 1993

	United States		Germany		France	
	Mean	Confidence Level (Different From Zero)	Mean	Confidence Level (Different From Zero)	Mean	Confidence Level (Different From Zero)
1-month stock return	-0.32%	99%	-0.26%	99%	-0.33%	99%
Book-to-price	0.14	99	0.16	99	0.18	99
12-month stock return	0.23	99	0.08	99	0.12	99
Cash flow-to-price	0.18	99	0.08	99	0.15	99
Earnings-to-price	0.16	99	0.04	83	0.13	99
Sales-to-price	0.08	99	0.10	99	0.05	99
3-month stock return	-0.01	38	-0.14	99	-0.08	99
Debt-to-equity	-0.06	96	-0.06	96	-0.09	99
Variance of total return	-0.06	94	-0.04	83	-0.12	99
Residual variance	-0.08	99	-0.04	80	-0.09	99
Five-year stock return	-0.01	31	-0.02	51	-0.06	94
Return on equity	0.11	99	0.01	31	0.10	99

Source: Reprinted from *Journal of Financial Economics,* 41, Robert Haugen and Nardin Baker, "Commonality in the Determinants of Expected Stock Returns," p. 433, Copyright 1996, with permission from Elsevier Science.

monthly return, and variability in stock return that is unexplained by movement in the market (residual variance).[2]

The relationship between risk and return seems to be upside down everywhere. Modern Finance gets it wrong in *every* country.

The fact that the list of familiar culprits in Table 8–1 keeps coming up in different time periods and now in different countries leads us to believe that these are among the true determinants of expected stock returns.

At this point the efficient market professors may wish to set forth the following counterargument.

Let's suppose that the true expected values for all the payoffs to all the factors were really *zero.*

Now let the five countries go through the global financial/economic environment of 1985 to 1993. Obviously unexpected developments will take place. These unexpected developments will make the average payoffs deviate from their expected values of zero. Given that all five countries went through the same global financial/economic environment, we should expect that the deviations from zero should be of the same sign.

Nice try.

Table 8–1 *(continued)*

	Great Britain		Japan	
	Mean	*Confidence Level (Different From Zero)*	*Mean*	*Conficence Level (Different From Zero)*
1-month stock return	-0.22%	99%	-0.39%	99%
Book-to-price	0.12	99	0.12	99
12-month stock return	0.21	99	0.04	86
Cash flow-to-price	0.09	99	0.05	91
Earnings-to-price	0.08	99	0.05	94
Sales-to-price	0.05	91	0.13	99
3-month stock return	-0.08	99	-0.26	99
Debt-to-equity	-0.10	99	-0.01	31
Variance of total return	-0.01	38	-0.11	99
Residual variance	-0.03	77	0.00	8
Five-year stock return	-0.06	96	-0.07	98
Return on equity	0.04	80	0.05	92

But this scenario works only if the realized payoffs are actually induced by common financial and economic forces. And, if this were true, the payoffs would be strongly correlated across countries.

Let's see how strongly correlated they really are.

We would expect the correlations to be highest across the European countries. Table 8–2 shows the correlations for the payoffs for the five most important factors of Table 8–1 for France, Germany, and Great Britain.

The correlations are, in fact, very low. Across all of the factors of Table 8–1 the average absolute value for the correlation coefficients is .105. We can conclude that commonality in the payoffs is *not* a product of a common financial/economic environment.

In Table 8–1, we see the true determinants of expected stock returns. They are common across countries because human beings populate each market—human beings with an inaccurate concept of the true length of the short run. Human beings that tend to overweight the most recent information received. Human beings that are subject to agency problems that plague the entire investment profession everywhere. Human beings that tend to mimic, with time, the fads of the investment profession in the leader of the financial world—the United States.

It is the commonalties in human behavior that create the commonality in the payoffs.

Table 8–2 Correlations between the Payoffs for the Six Most Important Factors

	Germany	France
1-Month Stock Return		
Germany		
France	0.264	
Great Britain	0.017	0.143
Book-to-price		
Germany		
France	0.169	
Great Britain	0.141	0.030
12-Month Stock Return		
Germany		
France	0.267	
Great Britain	0.096	0.124
Cash flow-to-price		
Germany		
France	−0.130	
Great Britain	−0.038	0.152
Earnings-to-price		
Germany		
France	0.032	
Great Britain	0.112	0.153
Sales-to-price		
Germany		
France	−0.032	
Great Britain	0.057	0.203

Source: Reprinted from *Journal of Financial Economics,* 41, Robert Haugen and Nardin Baker, "Commonality in the Determinants of Expected Stock Returns," p. 434, Copyright 1996, with permission from Elsevier Science.

PREDICTING INTERNATIONAL STOCK RETURNS

Our technique is identical to that described previously for the United States. Once again, in the first year, the factor payoffs are presumed to be zero for January. Those for February are presumed equal to those of January. Those for March are presumed equal to the average for January and February, and so on, until we can roll with 12.

And once again, the stocks are formed into deciles based on expected return.

The cumulative, realized rates of return are presented in Figures 8–1A through 8–1D.

Once again, the factor model has impressive predictive power.

To determine the impact of trading costs, we move to quarterly rebalancing and the construction of the L (low volatility), I (enhanced expected return), and H (high expected return) portfolios.

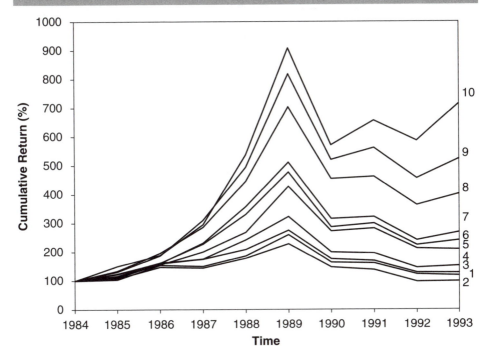

FIGURE 8–1A Cumulative Decile Performance, Japan

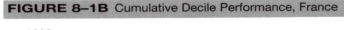

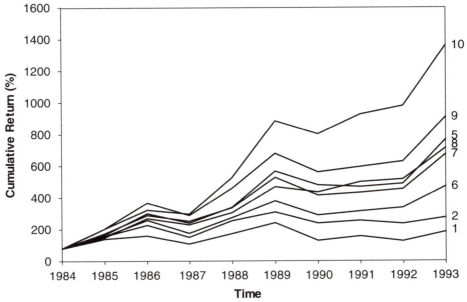

FIGURE 8–1B Cumulative Decile Performance, France

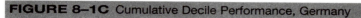

FIGURE 8–1C Cumulative Decile Performance, Germany

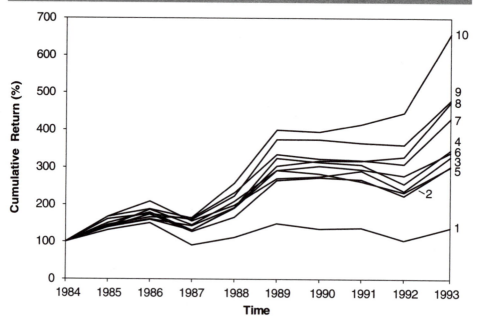

FIGURE 8–1D Cumulative Decile Performance, Great Britain

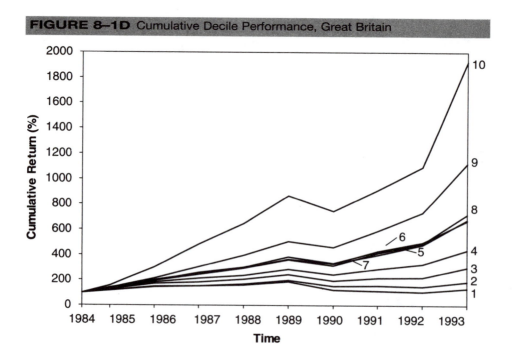

Figure 8–2 shows the performance (net of an assumed 2% round-trip transactions cost) of the capitalization-weighted index for each of the four foreign countries as well as the corresponding *G, I,* and *H* portfolios. Note that, in each country, the index is *inside* the efficient set.

In the upper left, we combine the five countries, including the United States, to create a global portfolio. The portfolio is rebalanced quarterly. We invest in each country in accord with its size. The stocks inside the country are selected in accord with the country's expected-return factor model and the optimization process.

The *H* portfolio now outperforms the capitalization-weighted index of the five countries by 5%.

FIGURE 8–2 Optimization in France, Germany, Great Britain, Japan and across the Five Largest Countries, 1985 to 1994

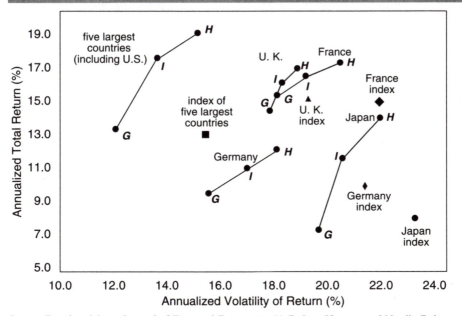

Source: Reprinted from *Journal of Financial Economics,* 41, Robert Haugen and Nardin Baker, "Commonality in the Determinants of Expected Stock Returns," p. 431, Copyright 1996, with permission from Elsevier Science.

AFTERTHOUGHTS

In this chapter the three countries of Europe were modeled individually. That is, the monthly payoffs for factors such as book-to-price were estimated separately for France, Germany and the United Kingdom. How would you expect the correlations between the payoffs to the various factors to look? Would you expect, for example, that the performance of cheap stocks is similar over time from country to country? Suppose, in the United States, that you separately estimated the payoffs to companies based in California and New York. In this case, you would expect the payoffs to be correlated over time, since stocks from both states are priced in an integrated stock market.

However, the payoffs to the stocks in the three European stocks do not exhibit a high level of correlation. In fact, until recently, the correlations were very low, indicating that the markets of Europe were not integrated. In a non-integrated setting, the individual countries are best modeled separately. However, as the European financial community integrates, payoff correlations can be expected to rise. Eventually, back tests should show that the predictive power of models that are estimated by co-mingling the stocks of Europe is higher than models where they are separated.

Notes

1. The statistical significance tells us the probability that the underlying expected payoffs to the factors are truly different from zero.

2. This is the same as diversifiable risk in a risk-factor model, where the market's return is the single factor.

PART II

WHY

9

THE TOPOGRAPHY OF
THE STOCK MARKET

ABNORMAL PROFIT

Running a business almost always requires a capital investment.

However, some require more than others. The capital investment is much more significant for a company that manufactures steel than for one that creates computer software.

Capitalists deserve a reasonable return on their investment. Reasonable, that is, given the *amount* of capital they must invest and the *risk* associated with the capital commitment.

Suppose you want to start an airline. You can initially get by on a $100 million investment. The 30-year Treasury bond is yielding 7%. You feel the stock market carries a 4% risk premium, but you also feel that an airline company carries twice the risk of an average stock. A 15% = (7% + 2 × 4%) return seems a fair return on your $100 million investment.

This means that you must *expect* that the airline's income, after all operating expenses (including a fair salary for you) and corporate income taxes, will net $15 million annually.

This $15 million would be your company's *normal* level of profits—an amount just sufficient to compensate you for the capital commitment and the risk you must bear in running the business.

Now, it may turn out that an airline is a better business than you expected. It may turn out that you make an annual profit of $20 million. If it actually turns out to be better, $5 million of the $20 million would be considered the annual *abnormal profit.*

Suppose you project an indefinite continuation of the current pleasant situation. The $5 million can then be considered a perpetual annuity. Its present value is computed as the annual annuity amount divided by a proper discount rate, which has already been determined to be 15%. Thus, the *present value* of your company's abnormal profits is $33.33 million ($5 million /.15).

Keep in mind that abnormal profits may also be negative. The airline business could have turned out to be *worse* than you expected.

TRUE AND PRICED ABNORMAL PROFIT

True Abnormal Profit is the *best* possible estimate of the present value of a company's future abnormal profits.

The best possible estimate is not necessarily highly accurate. It's simply the best estimate that can be made at the time. It is based on *all relevant information* currently available, and on the *best available technology* to process that information and make the forecast of future abnormal profits.

It's the most accurate forecast possible at the current time.

Now consider the estimate that's reflected in the price of your airline stock. Assume the market also believes that the $5 million will be a perpetual and level annuity. The market then prices your stock at $133.33 million, consisting of the $100 million present value of the normal profits ($15 million/.15) plus the $33.33 million present value of the abnormal profits.

In this case, the $33.33 million is called the *Priced Abnormal Profit*.

However, Priced Abnormal Profit is not necessarily equal to the true.

The market might be fooling itself that the annuity is perpetual. Your firm has a good deal going with the fat $20 million in annual net income. Other airlines may want to capture a piece of the action by requesting permission to fly your routes at lower prices. If so, you will have to lower *your* prices to meet *their* fares. You will suffer deterioration in both your profit margin and your share of the market.

Here, a *constant* level of abnormal profit probably isn't the best estimate. The best estimate should probably reflect an expected rate of decline in abnormal profits reflecting the true speed with which competitors will likely enter your business.

No decline is certainly unrealistic, but it *is* the assumption imbedded in the estimate reflected in our hypothetical market price.

In this case, the stock is selling at a Priced Abnormal Profit that's greater than the True.

THE EFFICIENT MARKET LINE

Figure 9–1 plots *Priced* Abnormal Profit on the horizontal scale and *True* Abnormal Profit on the vertical scale. Stocks below the horizontal have negative True Abnormal Profits. Stocks to the left of the vertical are priced as though they do.

The market gets it right if a stock sits on the 45-degree line labeled the *Efficient Market Line*. For all positions on this line, the estimate of abnormal profit reflected in the price is the best possible estimate. Those who believe in efficient markets think that no stock is ever positioned off this line.

If a stock is above the line, its True Abnormal Profit is larger than that reflected in its market price. As such, the stock is a bargain and should deliver an unexpectedly high rate of return in the future. Likewise, stocks

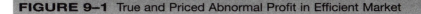

FIGURE 9–1 True and Priced Abnormal Profit in Efficient Market

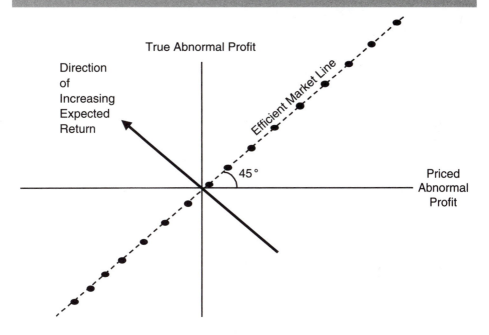

like your airline, positioned below the line, are overpriced. Their future returns will be deficient.

In general, expected returns increase as you move northwest on this market map. They remain constant as you move northeast or southwest, and they diminish as you move to the southeast.

IMPRECISION

Even the most ardent advocate of efficient markets wouldn't try to argue that all stocks are positioned exactly on a *line* in Figure 9–1.

It must be a *band.*

The question is—"How wide?"

This book makes a case that the band is *very* wide, as in Figure 9–2. Here the market prices stocks in a very sloppy fashion. It assigns the same price to stocks with different True Abnormal Profits. Likewise, it assigns different prices to stocks that have exactly the same True Abnormal Profits.

If the band is wide, then it is possible to beat the market by going west. Here you are looking for stocks that sell at relatively cheap prices but still have a reasonable profit potential.

You can also beat the market by going north—looking for stocks that have exceptional profit potential but still sell at reasonable prices.

FIGURE 9–2 The Position of Portfolios in Abnormal Profit Space

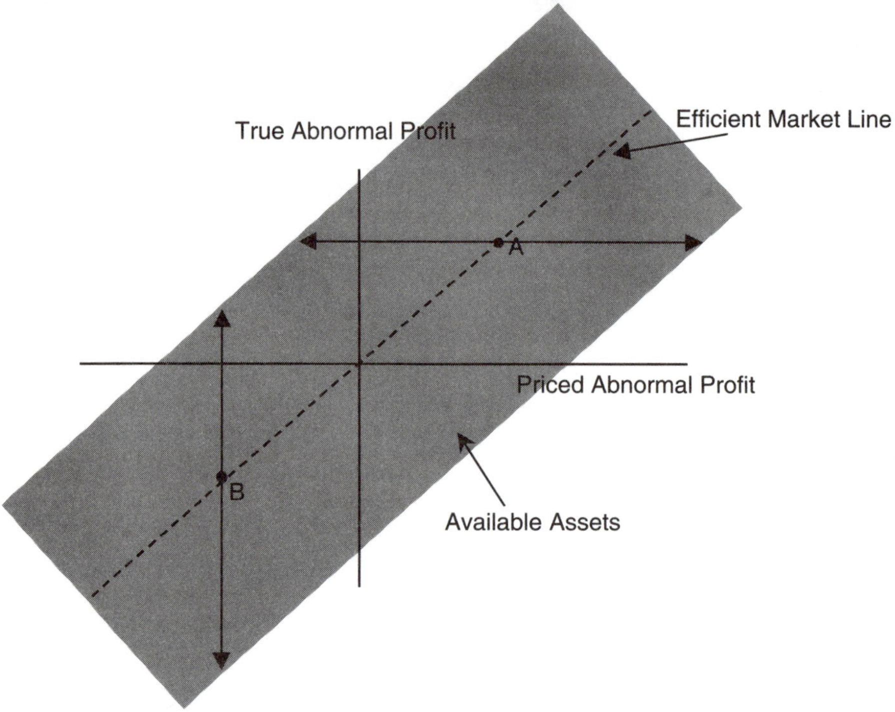

Note, however, that if you only went due north, trying to buy the most profitable companies without regard to the prices you must pay, you would expect to end up at a point like "A" in the *middle* of the band (left to right). In other words, you'd have some overpriced and some underpriced stocks in your portfolio, but, on average, you would expect to be positioned right on the Efficient Market Line. You wouldn't expect to out-perform in this case.

What would happen if you only went west? Went west looking for cheap stocks without regard to what condition the companies were in. This time, you expect to end up at a point like "B." By chance, you *will* buy some companies with positive abnormal profits, but most of your holdings will be negative abnormal profit firms. Once again, you'll have some underpriced and some overpriced stocks. But, on average, you can expect to be positioned in the middle of the band (top to bottom) on the Efficient Market Line. Again, no expected out-performance.

In this market, if you merely buy cheap stocks, your expected performance will be neutral.

That's interesting, because in *The New Finance,*[1] I present the results of many studies, all of which study the performance of stock portfolios formed by ranking stocks on the basis of some measure of Priced Abnormal Profit.[2] These studies uniformly find that portfolios containing cheap stocks have higher returns.

You wouldn't find this in the market of Figure 9–2.

For these findings, you need another form of market inefficiency.

Bias.

THE LENGTH OF THE SHORT RUN

In Econ. 101, our professors told us about the short run and the long run. Remember?

They said, "In the short run, the scale and nature of your plant and equipment are fixed, but in the long run, you can change even that."

They also said, "In competitive lines of business, you can earn abnormal profits in the short run, but in the long run, competitive forces will push your profits to normal levels."

You see, if your abnormal profits are positive, competitors will enter your line of business, forcing prices down and taking away your customers. If your abnormal profits are negative, competitors will leave. You can then claim their customers and raise your prices. This will allow your profits to return to a normal level.

A tendency for profits to mean-revert.

But, if you recall, our economics professors didn't tell us how long this process takes.

Just how long *is* the short run?

For the airline company we assumed it was *perpetual*.

Two questions:

How long does the market *think* it is.

And how long is it, *really?*

Three professional investors, Fuller, Huberts, and Levinson (FHL),[3] studied the second question. Looking at the roughly 1,000 largest firms in the United States over the period of 1973 through 1990, FHL ranked by earnings-to-price, and then created equally weighted quintiles, each containing 20% of the total.[4]

Presumably, the market expects the fastest growth from the 20% grouping with the lowest earnings-to-price ratio. For these firms, the current price is high relative to current earnings because the market believes earnings will be much higher in the future.

To see whether the market is correct in its expectation, FHL followed the actual average growth rates in earnings-per-share in the eight years following the formation of the quintiles.[5]

The results of their study are presented in Figure 9–3. Growth *relative to the middle quintile* is plotted on the horizontal axis. The year relative to quintile formation is plotted on the vertical.

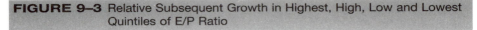

FIGURE 9–3 Relative Subsequent Growth in Highest, High, Low and Lowest Quintiles of E/P Ratio

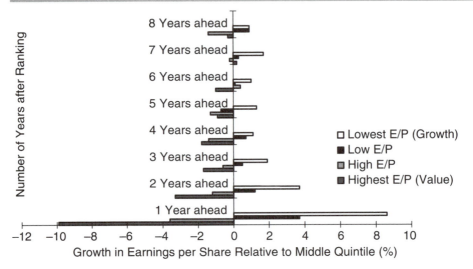

The market gets it right in the first year out. The lowest earnings-to-price quintile grew nearly 9% faster than the middle quintile. (If earnings for the middle grew at 5%, its earnings grew at nearly 14%.) Earnings for the highest quintile grew nearly 10% slower.

As we go into the second year and beyond, the identity of the firms in the quintiles remains constant. Thus, the black bar shows the growth in that year for the firms with the highest earnings-to-price ratios eight years before.

Note the high speed of mean-reversion in the growth rates. Four years out from quintile formation, there's very little difference in the growth rates.

The answer to the question, "How long is it, really?"

Three or four years.

But how long does the market *think* it is?

In *The New Finance,* I calculate the expected future total stock returns to the quintiles, given the measured speed of mean-reversion and the contemporary spread between the quintile earnings-to-price ratios. We calculate a spread of more that 6% between the *expected future rate of return* to the highest earnings-to-price quintile and the lowest.

And there is no evidence that the highest is more risky than the lowest.

The expensive stocks are expected to underperform, because the differentials in earnings yields are too wide relative to the true length of the short run. For the expensive stocks, $100 buys only a few dollars in current earnings. For the cheap stocks, $100 buys many more dollars in current earnings. With a high speed of mean-reversion in the growth rates for both, the earnings for the expensive stocks are never able to catch up.

Thus, the market, in its belief that they eventually will catch up, apparently thinks the short run is longer than it really is.[6]

BIAS

As in the example of the airline, if the market has an exaggerated view of the length of the short run, it will tend to overvalue positive abnormal profits, thinking they will persist for a longer period than is realistic. The absolute value of negative abnormal profits will be exaggerated in the price as well.

If exaggeration of the length of the short run is typical, this bias will have an important effect on the nature of our market map. Figure 9–4 shows a market characterized by both imprecision and the type of bias discussed here.[7] The band is now tilted down, with a slope less than 45 degrees. The greater the disparity between the market's belief and the actual length of the short run, the smaller the slope of the band.

This is a market consistent with the many results presented in *The New Finance.*

Rank stocks by some measure of Priced Abnormal Profit, then measure the performance of the stocks after the ranking. In Figure 9–4, the expensive stocks are, by construction, placed on the right-hand side of the horizontal. We expect them to fall in the (top to bottom) center of the band relative to True Abnormal Profit on the vertical—say, at point "A."

FIGURE 9–4 The Position of Portfolios in Abnormal Profit Space

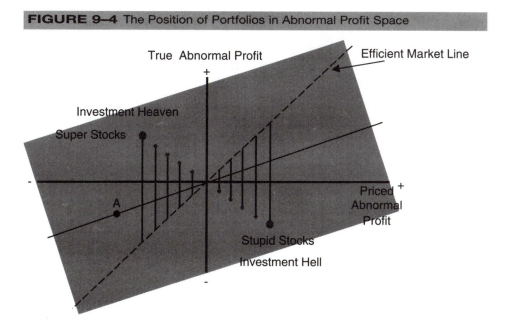

This position is under the Efficient Market Line, so the expensive stocks can be expected to under-perform, as they do in the studies documented in *The New Finance*.

Cheap stocks will be positioned to the left and also in the center of the band. They can be expected to out-perform — as they do.

You don't need *imprecision* to get these results, but you do need *bias*.

THE LANDS OF SUPER AND STUPID STOCKS

So how do Super and Stupid Stocks fit into this picture?

The lands of Super and Stupid Stocks were not previously thought to exist.

But they do.

The land of Super Stocks is located to the northwest in Figure 9–4. Portfolios in this area are both cheap and profitable. Although you can't see it in the figure, they are also relatively big, liquid, financially sound, and of low risk. And they are positioned well above the Efficient Market Line, poised to produce big returns in the future.

We shall call this land *Investment Heaven.*

Conversely, the land of Stupid Stocks lies to the southeast. Here, portfolios tend to contain stocks that are smaller and less liquid. The companies behind the stocks are in financial trouble. The stocks themselves tend to be volatile and risky. Being both expensive and unprofitable, these portfolios are positioned well under the Efficient Market Line, poised to produce very low returns in the future.

Call this land *Investment Hell.*

Recall from Figure 7–7 that the book-to-price ratios of the Super and Stupid Stock portfolios are approximately the same. In measures of cheapness, the Super and Stupid portfolios distinguish themselves on the basis of ratios like cash flow-to-price, earnings-to-price and dividend-to-price.

But not book-to-price.

The value/growth factor in the Fama-French risk-adjustment model *is* based on book-to-price. However, because most stocks are likely to be located in the northeast and southwest of Figure 9–4, stocks ranking low in book-to-price ratio are likely to be relatively profitable (as are Super Stock portfolios). Conversely, the high book-to-price stocks are likely to be relatively unprofitable (as are Stupid Stock portfolios). Because they are neutral with respect to book-to-price, it is their commonality with respect to relative profitability that causes the positive return relationships between Super and growth and between Stupid and value.

Having come to understand these aspects of the market's topography, we are now in a position to understand the payoffs to stocks that are cheap and to stocks that are profitable.

AFTERTHOUGHTS

In the closing years of the twentieth century, growth stocks have greatly out-performed value in terms of their price appreciation. Some have argued that the information revolution has created a new paradigm under which relatively profitable firms are now able to maintain their competitive positions much longer than before. Proponents of this view feel that the speed of mean-reversion depicted in Figure 9–3 is no longer in effect. Others, including this author, argue that the performance of growth stocks was a bubble, and that value stocks were more under-valued than ever.

In support of the bubble view, Chan, Karceski and Lakonishok[8] show that growth stocks, as a group, have not distinguished themselves in terms of profitability during the period over which they out-performed in terms of market price appreciation. In fact, large growth stocks have not out-performed large value stocks in terms of their growth in sales, operating income, or income available for distribution to common stockholders. Thus, while growth stocks have been priced as though they will be able to sustain their relative profitability, this assumption has not been validated by actual corporate performance even during the period over which they enjoyed superior performance in terms of their market prices.

Notes

1. R. Haugen, *The New Finance: The Case for an Over-reactive Stock Market,* Prentice Hall, 1998.
2. The various indicators are the ratios of book-to-price, earnings-to-price, and dividend-to-price.
3. R. Fuller, L. Huberts, and M. Levinson, "Returns to E/P Strategies, Higgledy Piggledy Growth; Analysts' Forecast Error, and Omitted Risk Factors," *Journal of Portfolio Management,* Winter, 1993.
4. FHL assume a three-month reporting lag for the earnings number. Thus, the ratio is computed as year-end earnings to price as of the end of March.
5. The quintiles are not re-formed during the eight-year period.
6. The complete case for this assertion is made in *The New Finance.*
7. If the market underestimated the length of the short run, the slope of the band would be greater than 45 degrees.
8. Chan L, J. Karceski, and J. Lakonishok, "A New Paradigm or the Same Old Hype?: The Future of Value Versus Growth Investing," *Unpublished Manuscript,* University of Illinois, March 2000.

10

THE POSITIVE PAYOFFS TO CHEAPNESS AND PROFITABILITY

WHAT'S BEHIND THE PAYOFFS

The cheapness family is the most powerful of the five.

This family exploits *both* imprecision and bias.

Suppose the market were merely imprecise, as in Figure 9–2. In this case, holding profitability constant as you move west to lower-priced stocks, you move up relative to the Efficient Market Line.

Recall our discussion of multiple regression in the context of the corner of the room in Chapter 3. As you slide the plane of best fit through the scatter of plot points in the room, you measure the payoff to one factor (cheapness) while holding constant the exposures and payoff to another factor (profitability).

Imprecision alone will create a positive payoff to cheapness. However, narrowing the width of the band will reduce the magnitude of the payoff. And if the band is reduced to a line, the component of the payoff to cheapness coming from market imprecision disappears entirely.[1]

However, even without a band, if the market overestimates the length of the short run, and a line in Figure 9–2 is sloped less than 45 degrees, the payoff to cheapness is still positive and inversely related to the slope of the line. As we see in Figure 10–1, a move to the west moves us up relative to the Efficient Market Line.

So the positive payoff to cheapness is supported by the market's imprecision *and* by its bias.

What's behind the payoff to profitability?

With no imprecision, the payoff to profitability is zero.

We owe the strong and significant positive payoffs to profitability to a high degree of market imprecision. When price is held constant, northerly movement within the band is associated with significantly higher return. If the band were too narrow, the payoff to profitability wouldn't be significantly positive.

FIGURE 10–1 The Position of Portfolios in Abnormal Profit Space

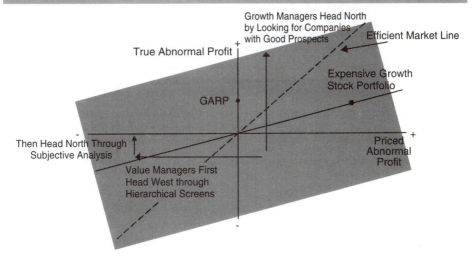

HOW GROWTH AND VALUE MANAGERS ADD VALUE FOR THEIR CLIENTS

Value managers typically use computerized databases and hierarchicaı screens.

When you employ a hierarchical screen, you rank stocks by some measure, and screen into a subpopulation, all of which rank high or low on the basis of the measure. A large-cap value manager might screen first on size, perhaps creating a subpopulation of the 500 largest stocks. Next, the manager screens the 500 on the basis of some measure of cheapness. The most popular measure is book-to-price, but many value managers screen on earnings-to-price or dividend-to-price. Some use a combination of indicators of cheapness. In any case, they screen from 500 down to perhaps 200 stocks, *all of which* are big and sell cheap in the market.

Through their hierarchical screens, value managers head for the west in Figure 10–1.

Then, most move from quantitative screens to a more subjective analysis.

They read trade magazines, make calls to investor-relations officers, read Wall Street research created by brokerage and investment banking firms, and analyze financial statements. They're trying to find firms that are selling cheap in the market but have reasonably good prospects nevertheless.

They're trying subjectively to move north in Figure 10–1.

We shall call this process "going around the corner."

Value managers attempt to get to Investment Heaven. But, as we shall later see, *you can't get to heaven by going around the corner.*

What about growth managers? What's *their* strategy?

Growth managers focus on *prospects*. Their evaluation process tends to be more subjective than that of a value manager. They look for companies with good management, exciting products, sound financials, and high profitability, as well as firms that are positioned well in their lines of business.

In terms of Figure 10–1, they are attempting to go north, taking advantage of the market's imprecision. Were it not for imprecision, there would be no role for growth managers. Without imprecision, even if the market got the length of the short run right, growth managers could only expect neutral performance, gross of fees and expenses.

We should distinguish between two very different types of growth managers.

The first type simply looks for the best companies *period*. Their investment philosophy is, "If you buy the companies with the very best prospects for success in their business, your performance is bound to be good in the long run."

Mistake.

In Figure 10–1, if you head north with no concern for the prices you're paying for the stocks you buy, you can expect to end up in the middle of the band (left to right).

Perhaps at the dot on the eastern part of the map, labeled "Expensive Growth Stock Portfolio."

This position is below the Efficient Market Line. Managers who buy the best at any price can expect to underperform. This is the type of manager who comes under criticism in *The New Finance*.

The second type of growth manager also looks for sound companies with good prospects. But these managers exercise price discipline. They are willing to invest only at reasonable stock prices.

This type of manager has a well-known acronym in the investment business:

GARP—*g*rowth *a*t a *r*easonable *p*rice.

The GARP manager is positioned above the Efficient Market Line at the central dot in Figure 10–1. By going north, without drifting too far to the east, GARP managers can expect to out-perform.

BENCHMARKING GROWTH AND VALUE MANAGERS

In the investment business, the investment performance of growth and value managers is usually measured relative to stylized benchmarks.

The stylized value index begins with the population of stocks in a particular generalized index such as the Russell 1000 Stock Index. This index is capitalization-weighted and contains the roughly 1,000 largest (based on market capitalization) U.S. equities. Russell ranks the 1,000 stocks on the basis of the ratio of book-to-market. Beginning with the stock with the highest ratio, Russell goes down the list to the midpoint in terms of total market capitalization. That is, the total market capitalization of the stocks in the top-side is equal to the total market capitalization of the stocks in the bottom-side of the list. The stocks in the top-side go in the Russell value index, and the stocks in the bottom-side go in the Russell growth index. Both indices are then capitalization-weighted.[2]

One frequently hears comments in the investment business that growth managers have an easier time out-performing their stylized benchmarks than do value managers.

A recently published empirical study by Coggin and Trzcinka[3] (CT) confirms this casual observation.

CT measure performance by relating the risk premiums[4] earned by growth and value managers to the risk premiums earned by their respective stylized benchmarks. They want to estimate the expected risk premium for the manager in market conditions where their benchmarks are producing no risk premium.[5] If the managers can be expected to produce a positive risk premium under these conditions, they can be said to be out-performing.

The results of the CT study are presented in Table 10–1.

For the growth managers, the out-performance averages roughly 4% annualized, with 130 out of 141 managers showing positive performance.

On the other hand, the value managers show less than 1% annualized added value relative to their index, with only 110 out of 170 out-performing. While the record of the value managers is good, it pales relative to the apparent performance of the growth managers.

Why?

In the context of Figure 10–2, the relative merits of growth and value investing are depicted by their positions relative to the Efficient Market Line. In the figure, I have assumed that growth and value investors are equally meritorious.

However, consider how they will perform relative to their stylized benchmarks.

The growth *benchmark,* constructed to contain expensive stocks, is positioned near the point labeled "Stylized Growth Benchmark." This

Table 10–1   Mean Alphas for Value and Growth Managers

Investment Model	Mean Alpha	No. Positive	No. Negative
Value	0.24%/Quarter	110	60
Growth	1.01%/Quarter	130	11

Source: T. Coggin and C. Trzcinka, "Analyzing the Performance of Equity Managers: A Note on Value Versus Growth," in *The Handbook of Equity Style Management,* (New Hope, PA: Frank Fabozzi Associates, 1997).

FIGURE 10–2 Growth and Value Managers and Their Benchmarks

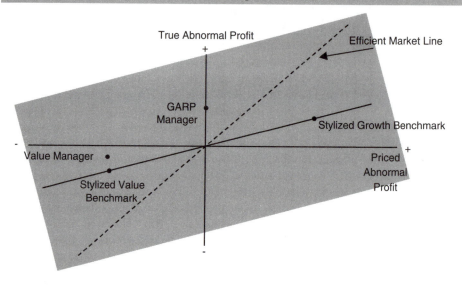

benchmark, being under the Efficient Market Line, can be expected to underperform. On the other hand, given their expected position, GARP managers can be expected to beat the general market. And they will easily out-perform their under-performing benchmark.

On the other hand, the value benchmark, made up of cheap stocks, is positioned above the Efficient Market Line at the point "Stylized Value Benchmark." Since this benchmark can be expected to out-perform, it will be difficult to beat. Value managers who beat it will do so by subjectively investing in stocks with good prospects in spite of the fact that they are selling cheap.

They can expect to beat their stylized benchmark only by successfully *going around the corner.*

When it comes to beating a stylized benchmark, there's only one type of growth manager that's in the same boat as the value managers (barring a successful attempt to subjectively move north)—growth managers who invest without price discipline.

AFTERTHOUGHTS

At the end of the previous chapter we discussed two views regarding the pricing of growth stocks at the end of the millennium. The prices of growth stocks have been bid up to unprecedented levels relative to earnings, cash flows, and dividends. Some take the view that these prices are justified because, based on the revolution in information technology, the mean reversion tendency in profitability that has existed in the past no longer holds under the new economic paradigm. Others believe that mean reversion, based on competitive entry and exit into lines of business, still holds as it did in the past, and growth stocks are more over-priced now than they have ever been. Let's call this the "bubble view."

Consider the slope of the band in Figure 10–1. How might the slope of the band look if we were truly operating under a new economic paradigm and growth stocks were rationally priced? Contrast this with the slope under the bubble view. We do know that the relative performance of value and growth stocks moves in a cycle. More often than not value out-performs growth, but there are periods, as we have recently seen, where growth stocks dominate. Think of the dynamics of the band of 10–1. How might changes in the slope of the band explain the cycle that we see in growth and value performance? Would the position, and changes in the position, of the band explain the cycle and the tendency of value to out-perform over the long-run?

Notes

1. Unless cheapness serves as a proxy for risk that increases the return *required* by investors.
2. The weighting is actually based on the fraction of the capitalization that is publicly traded, not the fraction that is privately held.
3. D. Coggin and C. Trzcinka, eds. "Analyzing the Performance of Equity Managers: A Note on Value Versus Growth," *The Handbook of Equity Style Management,* Frank Fabozzi Associates, New Hope, PA, 1997.
4. The difference between the monthly total return to the manager and the monthly return to U.S. Treasury bills.
5. Their estimate is the intercept for the regression of risk premiums.

11

THE NEGATIVE PAYOFF
TO RISK

Why do more risky stocks tend to have lower expected rates of return? This is easily the least intuitive of the findings of this book.

To figure out the answer, let's consider some of the things we've learned so far:

1. When significant, the payoffs to the risk factors average to negative numbers.
2. The portfolios of low-return Investment Hell contain relatively risky stocks.
3. The market index is deeply inside the efficient set and is easy to beat.

And it seems that it's common knowledge that:

4. Over the long term, the majority of investment professionals have had a difficult time beating the market index.

The first two findings state the puzzle itself. The last two provide clues to its answer.

HOW LONG HAS THIS BEEN GOING ON?

Remember the low-risk portfolio of Figure 5–5?

This portfolio is constructed by finding the particular portfolio weights that produce the lowest possible portfolio volatility over the trailing 24 months. The portfolio is rebalanced quarterly to this end.

If you recall, the low-risk portfolio actually outperformed the market index over the period 1979 through 1993. This, of course, is indicative of the negative payoff to risk *during this period.*

To see how long this has been going on, we will now track the relative performance of the low-risk portfolio over a much longer period. Figure 11–1 shows the cumulative *difference* in performance between the low-risk portfolio and the S&P 500 stock index since 1928.

Because the low-risk portfolio carries less risk than the market index, financial theory suggests it should have a lower expected return. On average, it *should* underperform the index. Thus, the cumulative difference in

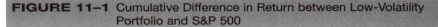

FIGURE 11–1 Cumulative Difference in Return between Low-Volatility Portfolio and S&P 500

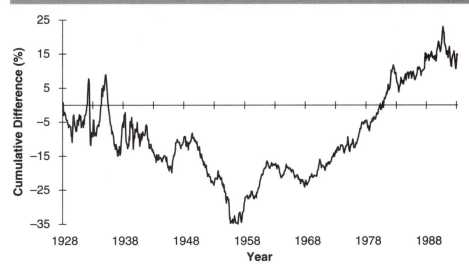

performance between the low-risk portfolio and the index should trend downward.

And it does.

At least until the late 1950s or early 1960s, when it reverses direction.

It so happens that the domination of the low-risk portfolio *begins* at the inception of two major events in the investment business:

1. The reappearance of growth-stock investing.
2. The dominance of the institutional investor.

Both events may serve to explain the negative payoff to risk.

GROWTH STOCKS AS OVERPRICED AND RISKY INVESTMENTS

Prior to the 1960s, growth stocks weren't a very popular form of investing. Rather, most believed in the investment philosophy presented in Graham and Dodd's *Security Analysis,* the book I studied in college.

Graham and Dodd warned against projecting earnings trends or growth rates into the future. In effect, they were telling us not to project a continuation of positive or negative abnormal profits into the future.

But in the 1960s, investors began to do just that. For them, beliefs in the length of the short run became longer and longer. It seems this was happening only in their minds. It would be very difficult to argue for coincident structural changes in industry that would be consistent with a general increase in the *true* length of the short run.

This being the case, the stocks experiencing positive abnormal profits (growth stocks) became overvalued, and the negative abnormal profit stocks (value stocks) became undervalued.

Much is expected from growth stocks and little from value stocks. Thus, one might expect a larger fraction of the market value of growth stocks would be buried in the distant future. If so, changes in expectations about the future would create larger percentage changes in the market values of growth stocks.

The returns to growth stocks *should* be more volatile.

And, evidence exists that growth stocks *are* more volatile.[1]

Suppose that, as we move through the volatility spectrum of the stock market, we tend to move through the abnormal-profit spectrum as well. Less-volatile stocks tend to have negative abnormal profits; more-volatile stocks tend to have positive abnormal profits.

This being the case, realized returns should tend to fall as the relative volatility of a stock increases.

So growth stocks tend to be more volatile. But expensive growth stocks also tend to be overpriced and tend to produce unexpectedly low returns in the future.

In this market, investors *want* to be rewarded for bearing greater relative risk in the stock market. But they are, consistently and systematically, unpleasantly surprised by the low returns to expensive stocks that also tend to be more volatile.

Their expectations for the rewards of bearing risk are overridden, again and again, by the performance consequences of overestimating the length of the short run.

This is the first explanation.

Now, the second.

INTRIGUE

Imagine that you are a security analyst at a major investment firm.

You specialize in three related industries. In fact, your former job was that of a marketing analyst in one of them. You read the trade journals. You go to trade shows and forums. You talk to your former colleagues and competitors. You develop a list of firms that aren't in the core portfolio, but that you, nevertheless, find attractive. You also have a list of stocks that *are* in the portfolio, but that, in your eyes, are beginning to fall from grace.

As an analyst, a crucial part of your job is making recommendations to your investment committee, which consists of three senior partners in the firm and the chief investment officer—your boss. Every Friday, you go before this committee with several recommendations of stocks to buy or sell.

The committee's job is to assess the merits of your recommendations and to keep the portfolio in balance. To keep it diversified in its bets on stocks, industries, and sectors.

Can you imagine what would happen to you if the committee viewed the great majority of your recommendations with skepticism and disbelief? Yes, they would accept some of your "buys" out of the need to keep in balance, but your credibility would remain marginal.

You would eventually be fired.

Individuals don't have to make a case for the stocks they invest in, but *fiduciaries* do.

They must defend their decisions to investment committees, portfolio managers, and most important, to their clients. They must come up with *compelling* reasons why the stocks they like are particularly attractive.

It is easier to make a compelling case for a company that is inherently *interesting,* like a company that is marketing new and exciting products. A company with innovative marketing and management strategies, run by a charismatic, outspoken, and well-known CEO, or a company with an active and innovative mergers and acquisitions program is exciting and intriguing.

You can more easily make a case for the companies you can spin investment themes and stories around: companies the people of Wall Street are talking about, companies you've just read about in *The Wall Street Journal* or *Business Week;* companies in the news. Part of your case can then be based on what you read in the news.

Given a choice between an intriguing and exciting company and a stodgy, boring company that nobody is currently concerned about, you'll take the interesting one before the committee every time.

Because you have to make their cases, you have a preference for *interesting and exciting* stocks. Many investors call these story stocks.

These are the stocks that people are talking about. These are the ones in the news.

On some days, the news is good, and the stocks go up. Other days, it's bad, and they go down.

You see, *volatility comes along with excitement.*

Because fiduciaries have these agency problems, they may look at risk differently than the clients they represent. Yes, they know their high-net-worth clients don't care for volatility, but that investment committee must be faced week after week. Remember, if they don't like your stories, it's your quickest path out the door.

Besides, most of the firm's clients aren't individual investors. They're pension funds. Pension boards don't care much about the volatility of any one of their managers. They diversify across many managers. What they care about is whether they can expect any one manager to outperform their benchmark. If they don't have *that* expectation, *then* they fire the manager.

So who cares if volatility comes along with excitement?

Recent evidence supports the contention that institutional investors may be attracted to volatile stocks. Results of a recent paper by Sias[2] are presented in Table 11–1.

Table 11–1 Median institutional holdings, capitalization, and volatility by capitalization: Institutional holdings sorted portfolios, NYSE firms, 1977 to 1991

| | Institutional Holdings (%) | | |
| | | | Confidence Level (High Minus Low) |
Portfolio	High	Low	
Smallest	0.2275	0.2144	99%
Decile 2	0.3335	0.3082	99
Decile 3	0.3978	0.3623	99
Decile 4	0.4760	0.4277	99
Decile 5	0.5268	0.4510	99
Decile 6	0.5564	0.4558	99
Decile 7	0.5916	0.4390	99
Decile 8	0.6361	0.4408	99
Decile 9	0.6566	0.3887	99
Largest	0.6428	0.3455	99

Sias studied all stocks listed on the New York Stock Exchange from 1977 through 1991. For each year, he ranked the stocks by total market capitalization and formed the stocks into size deciles. Sias then gathered information as to the percentage of outstanding shares held by institutions in the third quarter of each year. He also computed the volatility of each stock for the year, using weekly returns.

For each size decile, Sias ranked the stocks on the basis of the fraction of the shares institutionally held and divided the stocks into three groups of equal numbers—high, medium, and low.

Then he compared the high and the low institutional holding groups in terms of: (a) percentage institutional holdings, (b) average market capitalization, and (c) average volatility of return for the stocks in the groups.

Table 11–1 shows that, while institutions are primarily in the larger stocks, the *difference* between the institutional holdings in the low and high groups doesn't show a trend as you go from the smallest to the largest stocks.

As one might expect, within each size decile, institutions tend to be in the larger capitalization stocks. And, interestingly, within each size decile, they tend to be in the more *volatile* stocks.

We now confront a question of causation. Are the institutions in the more volatile stocks because they are attracted to volatility?

Or does the causation go the other way? Are the stocks more volatile because the institutions are trading them in large blocks? The large trades

Table 11–1 *(continued)*

Capitalization ($ millions)			Annualized Standard Deviation of Weekly Returns (%)		
High	*Low*	*Confidence Level (High Minus Low)*	*High*	*Low*	*Confidence Level (High Minus Low)*
28.5600	18.5600	99%	43.27	49.47	99%
60.4600	52.1500	99	36.70	32.81	99
91.8700	84.0450	99	36.49	30.86	99
151.1000	135.2500	99	35.05	29.85	99
222.3500	207.4500	99	33.39	28.70	99
364.4500	326.8000	99	32.02	25.56	99
562.8000	514.9000	99	30.65	27.19	99
926.7500	838.2000	99	29.21	25.38	99
1,629.0000	1,491.5000	99	28.34	24.52	99
3,777.0000	4,338.5000	99	26.03	23.80	99

might be causing price pressure, and the price pressures might create the differences in volatility that we see in the table.

Sias opted for the second explanation, but his data supports the first.

One would expect any alleged disruption caused by institutional price pressure to be *much* stronger for the smaller stocks, but the average difference in volatility is 4.07% for the five largest deciles and only 2.64% for the smallest five. This is the case, although the difference in institutional ownership between low and high is about the same across the size deciles.

I conclude from this that the more likely direction of causation is from volatility to institutional ownership and not from institutional ownership to volatility.

In summary, fiduciaries like the intrigue and excitement that accompanies volatility. The agency problem associated with their keen desire to make a case for their stocks may result in raising the prices of risky stocks to the point where they no longer produce risk premiums for their investors. This is the second explanation for the negative payoff to risk.

Understand that the two explanations are noncompeting; that is, *both* may account for the negative payoff to risk that we have observed since the early 1960s.

Interestingly, these explanations may also partially account for the many studies[3] that show poor performance among institutional investors over the long term. If institutional investors are attracted to growth stocks and stocks with intriguing and exciting prospects, we should expect them to underperform. The prices of both have been driven up to the point where they are overvalued.

Fiduciaries may be the *victims* of the impact of their own agency problems on market inefficiency.

AFTERTHOUGHTS

As alluded to in the previous two chapters, the relative performance of growth stocks was very strong in 1998 and 1999. Based on what we learned in this chapter, it should not be surprising to you that stocks with higher market betas produced relatively high returns during the same period as well. Does this mean that we can expect the payoff to risk to be positive in the future? The payoff to risk *was* positive in 1990, 1991, and 1995, but it was once again negative in years 1992, 1993, 1994, 1996, and 1997. Recall the "bubble" vs. "new paradigm" views presented at the end of the last chapter. How might these alternative views bear on the question of the long-term future of the risk-return relationship?

Notes

1. See Table II of E. Fama and K. French, "The Cross-Section of Expected Stock Returns," *Journal of Finance,* June 1992: 436–37. The table clearly shows that stocks with higher betas tend to have lower book-to-price ratios.

2. R. Sias, "Volatility and the Institutional Investor," *Financial Analysts Journal,* March-April 1996.

3. See, for example, J. Lakonishok, A. Shleifer, and R. Vishny, "The Structure and Performance of the Money Management Industry," *Brookings Papers: Macroeconomics,* 1992.

12

THE FORCES BEHIND THE TECHNICAL PAYOFFS TO PRICE HISTORY

As discussed in Chapter 4, the expected-return factor model detects three distinct patterns in the history of stock returns that are predictive of the future.

First, we see *short-term reversal* patterns. If the performance of a stock was strong in the past one to six months, that's predictive of relatively poor performance in the next month. Conversely, poor past performance predicts a strong future.

Second, we see *intermediate-term inertia*. Strong performance in the past twelve months is indicative of relatively strong performance in the next month. And weak predicts weak.

Finally, there are *long-term reversal* patterns. If a stock did well in the course of the last three to five years, that bodes poorly for the next month. On the other hand, poor performance is a good sign.

Why?

SHORT-TERM REVERSALS

Short-term reversals in stock returns were discovered by Jegadeesh.[1]

In coming up with a rationale for their existence, we must first consider the possibility that they are merely an artifact of the Bid-Asked Bounce discussed in Chapter 6. Remember, since the closing price for the month is at the bid, the closes at the end of the *previous* month and the end of the *next* month have an equal chance of being at the asked. Thus, we may see a "down-then-up" pattern in the returns, even when there is no pattern actually there.

Jegadeesh supposedly accounted for this by removing the first trading day of the month from his returns. Just as we found that the predictive power of our model remained intact after removing a month between prediction and execution, he found that last month's return was predictive of next month's relative return even after removing the trading day.

Why would strong performance be closely followed by weak performance and vice versa?

Jegadeesh suggests price pressure. For example, someone tries to buy a lot of the stock, depleting the dealer's inventory. To meet the demand, the dealer raises the bid price, so as to attract more of the stock. The price is temporarily suspended above its equilibrium value. Investors, who were only marginally comfortable with holding the stock before, now sell it, pushing the price back to equilibrium, creating a short-term reversal pattern.

Although this sequence of events seems to make sense on the surface, it seems strange that the reversals last as long as they do.

So we look to another explanation. Perhaps the market overreacts to more than records of recent success and failure on the part of firms (overestimating the length of the short run).

Perhaps it overreacts to many things.

Behaviorists tell us that we tend to overweight and overreact to the most recently received information. If we do, we will find that the information that we thought was so important becomes *tempered,* and *reduced in significance,* by new and related information that follows.

If the market's reaction to the initial information was unbiased, one would expect the new, related information to have an equal chance to send the stock price in the opposite direction from its response to the initial information. However, if the market overweighted the initial information, then the odds would favor a reversal. If the initial information were positive, the price rises to reflect an overly optimistic prediction of events to follow. Thus, there is a greater-than-equal chance of a future negative surprise: overreactions followed by corrections.

This may be a more plausible explanation for the very strong one-to-three-month reversal patterns embedded in stock returns.

INTERMEDIATE-TERM INERTIA AND LONG-TERM REVERSALS

These patterns appear to be related to *surprises* in the magnitudes of reported earnings.

The evidence for this is clear in a study by Jegadeesh and Titman (JT).[2]

Studying stocks on the New York and American Exchanges for the period 1980 through 1989, JT ranked stocks on the basis of their performance over the preceding six months. They focused on the 10% of the stocks that did the best (the winners) and the 10% that did the worst (the losers).

They then observed the price reactions of the winners and the losers to earnings reports in the following 36 months.

Table 12–1 shows the difference in the returns to winners and losers in the three-day interval that includes the two days before and the day of the

Table 12-1 Differences in Return (and Confidence Levels) between Winners and Losers Around Earnings Announcement Dates

Month Following Decile Formation	Difference between the Returns to Winners and Losers	Month Following Decile Formation	Difference between the Returns to Winners and Losers	Month Following Decile Formation	Difference between the Returns to Winners and Losers
1	0.0055 (99%)	13	−0.0055 (98%)	25	−0.0002 (8%)
2	0.0082 (99%)	14	−0.0080 (99%)	26	−0.0021 (68%)
3	0.0082 (99%)	15	−0.0071 (99%)	27	−0.0032 (90%)
4	0.0090 (99%)	16	−0.0097 (99%)	28	−0.0028 (80%)
5	0.0059 (99%)	17	−0.0062 (99%)	29	−0.0015 (46%)
6	0.0058 (99%)	18	−0.0060 (99%)	30	−0.0021 (72%)
7	0.0013 (46%)	19	−0.0031 (89%)	31	−0.0027 (86%)
8	0.0000 (1%)	20	−0.0017 (58%)	32	−0.0021 (73%)
9	−0.0020 (71%)	21	0.0006 (21%)	33	−0.0020 (70%)
10	−0.0031 (88%)	22	−0.0005 (22%)	34	−0.0017 (63%)
11	−0.0039 (97%)	23	−0.0001 (4%)	35	−0.0022 (80%)
12	−0.0053 (99%)	24	0.0012 (46%)	36	−0.0059 (99%)

Source: N. Jegadeesh and S. Titman, "Returns to Buying Winners and Selling Losers: Implications for Stock Market Efficiency," *Journal of Finance,* 48, March 1993, Copyright American Finance Association. Reprinted with permission.

earnings announcement.[3] Reading the table, in the first month following the ranking, winners outperformed losers by 55 basis points. Statistically, we can say that the winners outperformed in this month with 99% confidence.

Reactions to the reports continue to be relatively positive for the winners for the next six months. The winners seem to be experiencing positive earnings surprises and the losers negative.

Why?

The answer lies in the properties of the earnings numbers generated by the accounting profession.

A good earnings report appears to serve as a signal for one or two more to come with the converse for a bad report.[4] The inefficient market doesn't seem to be aware of this.[5]

The winners undoubtedly reported good earnings in the six-month performance measurement period. That's why they won. The losers probably reported bad earnings.

An efficient market would have seen the good and bad reports as precursors for a few more to come. It would have completed its reaction with the announcement of the first report. The inefficient market doesn't understand this. It is surprised by the continuation.

This is the source of the intermediate-term inertia in stock returns.

Then, as the links in the chain connect, it *overreacts,* not just during the days surrounding the reports, but in-between the reports as well. As the chain initially extends, the market projects it to continue to extend for many years into the future.

It projects a *long* short run.

Too long.

Then, as we get into the ninth month and beyond in Table 12–1, the market becomes unpleasantly surprised by the reports of the winners. In the ninth month, we can say with 71% confidence that the losers, on average, out-perform. It had priced them based on a projection that the earnings would continue to grow at rapid rates for an extended period. The competitive forces of mean-reversion are setting in more quickly than expected. Stock prices fall with the receipt of each disappointing earnings report.

The opposite is happening with the losers. Instead of continuing to suffer as expected, they too mean-revert. Quick recovery is unexpected; their stock prices rise with each unexpectedly good report.

This is the source of the long-term reversal patterns in stock returns.

But wait!

Feel the tremor.

The earth shakes.

Quickly! Place your ear to the ground.

The army of Modern Finance is coming once again, marching into another battle.

AFTERTHOUGHTS

We have seen the predictive patterns in stock prices change as the period over which we measure returns in the past goes from long to short. Good returns over the last three to five years are ominous. Good returns over the last twelve months are a positive sign. Good returns over the last one to six months are again ominous.

Might this pattern continue if we measure the past return over an even shorter interval? Suppose the market isn't instantaneous in reacting to announcements of information. Or suppose that a change in the price of one stock triggers successive changes in the prices of others, which in turn reinforces and induces further changes in the original stock. In the presence of these market tendencies, how might returns over the past few days or even hours be predictive of the future?

In this book we discussed a factor model that predicts returns over the next month. What if we shortened the horizon and attempted to predict returns over the next week? What additional factors might we need in our model? What would be your guess as to the impact of shortening the horizon on the relative importance of technical, price-history factors relative to fundamental factors such as return-to-equity or book-to-price?

Notes

1. N. Jegadeesh, "Evidence of Predictive Behavior in Stock Returns," *Journal of Finance,* 1990.

2. N. Jegadeesh and S. Titman, "Returns to Buying Winners and Selling Losers," *Journal of Finance,* March 1993.

3. Because firms report quarterly, an average of one-third of the firms are included in the return measurement for each month.

4. J. Wiggens, "Do Misconceptions about the Earnings Process Contribute to Post-Announcement Drift," *Working Paper,* Cornell University, Ithaca, New York.

5. V. Bernard and J. Thomas, "Evidence that Stock Prices Do Not Fully Reflect the Implications of Current Earnings for Future Earnings," *Journal of Accounting and Economics,* 1990.

13

COUNTERATTACK —
THE SECOND WAVE

Now the army appears on the horizon. The mighty army of Modern Finance.

But what kind of an army is this? They're not marching. In fact, they appear to be downright drunk, drinking champagne and celebrating!

Ten thousand professors, led by three colleagues—Brennan, Chordia, and Subrahmanyam (BCS)—riding on a donkey, the other professors are setting palm leaves before the donkey's path and chanting, "Hail the Divine Saviors! Hail to the authors of the Great Paper.[1] The greatest paper in the history of Modern Finance. Modern Finance is once again secure and most powerful. The anomalies are forever swept away.[2] Hail, Hail!"

These guys don't want to fight. They're so happy they're actually delirious!

And they're claiming victory. They think the war is *over*.

What's this all about anyway?

CASTRATING A FACTOR MODEL

After declaring the results upon which this book is based "a formidable challenge to factor: pricing theory," BCS attempt to build their own factor model and, with it, get to their analog of our Table 4–1.

Using portfolios constructed from an average of 980 NYSE stocks per month, BCS estimate their model in each month over the period 1977 through 1989.

Table 13–1 shows some of their results. As in our Table 4–1, the mean values for the payoffs to their factors are presented, along with the probabilities that the means are truly different from zero.

The first two sets of columns show the results when the model is estimated using 25 equally weighted portfolios of approximately 40 stocks each. The portfolios are formed by first ranking the 980 stocks with respect to size and dividing them into size quintiles. Then, within each quintile, the portfolios are ranked with respect to book-to-price ratios and divided into five book-to-price quintiles, for a total of 25 portfolios.

Table 13–1 Average Payoffs to the BCS Factor Model

Factor	Portfolio Returns		Residual Portfolio Returns		Residual Stock Returns	
	Mean Payoff	Confidence Level (%)	Mean Payoff	Confidence Level (%)	Mean Payoff	Confidence Level (%)
Size	.205	93	−.092	80	_.442	99
Book-to-Market	.730	98	.559	80	−.256	99
Volume of Trading	−.033	60	−.231	80	−.108	90
Number of Analysts Covering	−.023	20	−.166	65	.214	99
Dispersion of Earnings Estimates	−.050	70	−.694	92	−.287	99
Bid-Asked Spread (%)	1.020	99	.259	6	−.534	99
Institutional Ownership (%)	−.211	80	.448	98	.179	99
1.00 if in S&P; 0 Otherwise	−.107	10	.734	93	.184	95
Reciprocal of Share Price	−.006	5	.301	65	.069	60
Dividend-to-Price	−9.38	93	−3.70	65	2.33	85
2-Month Past Return	−.300	80	−2.18	80	−.280	20
5-Month Past Return	.150	75	−.268	20	−.929	80
11-Month Past Return	.430	99	1.56	93	.778	97

For the third set of columns, the model is estimated over the 980 individual stocks.

Look at the probabilities that the underlying expected payoffs are really different from zero. Not nearly as impressive as our Table 4.1, is it?

BCS aren't looking to impress. They *want* their results to look bad. They want to show that the only determinants of stock returns are *proper* variables—variables consistent with the theories of Modern Finance.

All the professors are very happy with these results. Break out the champagne!

But why *are* their results so different from ours? Yes, they've got about a third of the population used by us, and they don't include many of the variables we included, but surely *that* can't account for such a big difference.

No, it's the *other things* that account for it.

What other things?

Let's first examine the results in the first set of columns. Here the BCS factor model was used to explain the monthly differences in the *rates of return* to the 25 stock portfolios. But in *our* model, we had 3,000 observations to work with. Here, in each month, there are only the 25 portfolio returns. And they are trying to explain the differences in 25 returns with 13 factors.

Remember the corner of the room with the plot points suspended in the air? Let's make some good use of that corner right now.

Imagine how reliable your estimates of the slopes would be if you tried to slide a plane of best fit through only *four plot points?* Proportionately, that's what's being done here.

In addition, these portfolios are *designed* to be heterogeneous with respect to book-to-price and size. However, because the portfolio exposures to the *other* factors are the unranked averages of the exposures of 40 stocks, the portfolios are likely to be much more homogeneous with respect to these. In terms of the corner of the room, for the unranked factors, the four plot points will be positioned *in close proximity to one another relative to the two walls.*

To see this, suppose we select 40 of the 980 stocks at random to be included in an equally weighted portfolio. First think of the room with the 40 points we selected scattered in space. Now imagine computing the average value of the 40 points with respect to their exposure relative to the factor on the right wall. Now do the same thing for the left wall. The average factor values will probably fall above a point on the floor, near the middle of the room.

Select 40 more stocks at random, and it is likely that you'll get a similar result. Data points for factors not used in the ranking process for portfolio formation are likely to be located near the population averages.

Now consider the difference for data points that come from portfolios ranked on the basis of size and book-to-price.

Suppose we're plotting size along the left wall and book-to-price along the right. Here the 25 portfolios are formed by ranking on each factor, one at a time. Because of this, each portfolio has a distinctly different size and book-to-price ratio. The plot points will be scattered throughout the room, and we are more likely to find significant slopes for the plane of best fit along the two walls.

In this regard, note that the payoff to book-to-market is positive and highly significant.[3] The mean payoff to size is also relatively significant, although size doesn't make *our* top-ten list (Table 4–1) in any case.

In spite of the use of portfolios to estimate the model, we also see evidence of the presence of some of our friends from Part I—short-term reversals, intermediate-term inertia, and negative payoffs to liquidity.

But we now know why the results of the first set of columns don't look nearly as good as the results in our Table 4–1.

Let's move on to the second set of columns in Table 13–1.

These also look bad.

Same problems here as in the first set of columns: too few data points, exposures averaged over 40 heterogeneous stocks to come up with homogeneous averages.

But something else is going on as well.

You see, *here* the factor model isn't being used to explain differences in *rates of return.* Rather, it's being used to explain *residual returns,* net of another factor model.

An APT type model.

BCS use a statistical procedure[4] to find five factors that fully explain the correlations between the returns to the 980 stocks over the period of their study. In our previous discussion of APT, the factors were real variables like industrial production, inflation, and interest rates. In the case of BCS, the factors are *stock portfolios* and the payoffs are the *monthly returns* to the portfolios.

The five stock portfolios are constructed so that the correlations between their returns fully account for the correlations *between* the returns to the 980 stocks.

BCS also estimate the APT betas for each stock over the period of their study.[5]

They then subtract, from each stock's monthly return, the five components of the return accounted for by each of the five portfolios (the product of the stock's portfolio beta and the APT portfolio's monthly return). This gives them the stock's *residual, or diversifiable, return* for the month—the part of the stock's return that is unaccounted for by the returns to the five APT portfolios.

Thus, for the second set of columns of Table 13–1, the *systematic components* of their returns have been removed from the returns to these 40-stock portfolios.

Now please take another look at Figure 3–3. Remember the glide path? It shows what happens to diversifiable risk as you increase the number of stocks in an equally weighted portfolio.

In terms of Figure 3–3, BCS, *with a 40-stock portfolio,* would be off the graph to the far right. *There's likely to be little or nothing left of the residual return to be explained by the factor model.*

Let's call this the "Impotence by Castration" the IC technique.

BCS are trying to explain the diversifiable components of return for well-diversified portfolios.

In well-diversified portfolios, the diversifiable components of return are *miniscule.*

That's why the results of the second set of columns don't compare with our Table 4–1—it's the IC technique!

In the final set of columns in Table 13–1, the diversifiable components of the returns to the 980 *individual stocks* are used to estimate the factor model. For individual stocks, the diversifiable components of return are large relative to well-diversified portfolios. Note that many of the mean values for the factor payoffs are now significantly different from zero.

The IC technique wasn't used here. These numbers are taken from the beginning of the glide path (1 stock) and not from the far right (40 stocks).

Once again, I'm very impressed with these objective defenders of Modern Finance.

I think the IC technique is worthy of induction into the Hall of Divine Saviors at the Holy Temple of Efficient Markets. Once inducted, it will sit on a gold pedestal next to the pedestals belonging to the Fama-French risk-adjustment model and the Preposterous Private Information Hypothesis of French and Roll.[6]

Servatorem meum in basem auream pono, in magnoatrio Servatorum.

I predict that we will see more *bad* expected-return factor models published by the defenders of Modern Finance. You see, just as with anything else, it's easy to build bad factor models. If you're against airplanes, build planes that will crash. Then crash them, and tell people we don't really know how to fly, so don't get into airplanes.

The war is far from over. Take those drunks as prisoners. These professors should prepare to *fight*.

Fairly.

We now challenge them to a *race* of predictive power. We say we can predict better than the theories of Modern Finance. *Much* better.

The professors of Modern Finance are, once again, laughing up their sleeves. Don't we know that back-testing predictive models is *gauche*. They would rather compare the mathematical elegance of their models with that of ours.

We've got some news for them.

In real-world Finance, they don't pay for elegance. They pay for power—*predictive power.*

So, gauche or not, let's see who predicts best.

THE GREAT RACE

The three contestants in the race will be CAPM, APT, and an expected-return factor model of The New Finance. All will be run over the same time period, 1980 through 1999, and over a similar stock population—roughly the largest 3,500 stocks in the United States, as used in the tests of Chapter 5.

The New Finance will require fundamental accounting data. Its run will assume a three-month reporting lag from the start through 1987. After 1987, the actual data files that were available at the time will be used to compute the exposures needed to calculate expected rates of return.

The track is well groomed, an even playing field. The New Finance is first to the starting line.

No elegant theory here. Our model is *ad hoc,* but we're confident that it's powerful at predicting nevertheless.

In the race, we will enter a contestant similar to that discussed in Chapter 4. New variables are used related to reported-earnings surprise and predicted-earnings revisions, but the model is basically pretty much the same as described in this book.

Expected returns are calculated as the sum of the products of the projected factor payoffs (the average of the trailing 12 months) and the factor exposures going into the month. The stock population is ranked by expected return and formed into deciles. The deciles are reformed monthly. As with the runs for the other two contestants, transaction costs will not be accounted for. This is purely a test of predictive power.

The starter's gun is fired; the computer begins to spin. After several hours, the run is finished.

The results for The New Finance are presented as cumulative returns for the deciles in Figure 13–1.

Very impressive, I'd say. The average annual returns to the deciles are plotted in Figure 13–2. The spread between one end of the line-of-best-fit through the ten plot points is 37.17%. And the percentage of the differences in the overall returns to the deciles explained by decile number is 94%.

All in all, an impressive display of predictive power.

The New Finance steps aside and the first entrant for Modern Finance, CAPM, confidently sets itself in the starting blocks.

After all, it *did* win the Nobel Prize.

As we learned in Chapter 2, CAPM predicts that market beta is the sole determinant of expected stock return. We compute beta by regressing each stock's return on the S&P 500's return over the trailing 48–60 months, depending on data availability. Betas are recalculated every month; the

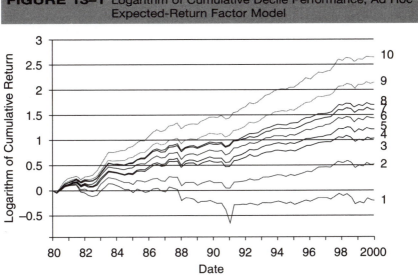

FIGURE 13–1 Logarithm of Cumulative Decile Performance, Ad Hoc Expected-Return Factor Model

FIGURE 13–2 Decile Returns for the Ad Hoc Factor Model

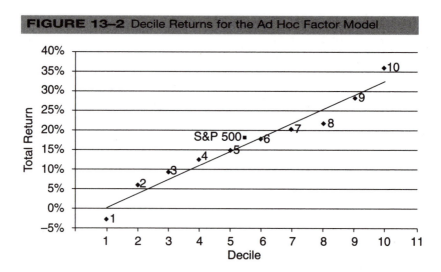

stocks are ranked by trailing beta and formed into deciles. Decile 10 has the stocks with the largest beta, and, therefore, the stocks with the highest expected returns. Decile 1, the lowest.

Once again, the starter's gun sounds, and CAPM is off and running. Being relatively simple and, of course, *more elegant,* CAPM finishes its run more quickly.

The results are presented in Figure 13–3.

Absolutely disgusting!

The average annual returns, by decile, are shown in Figure 13–4. The slope of the line-of-best-fit is negative with a spread of −5.67% between one end of the line and the other. The 1980s weren't good to CAPM. It had 10 years of successive negative spreads from 1981 through 1990, averaging −11.6%.

One last time: "The payoff to risk-bearing is *negative* in the stock market."

As CAPM crawls off in shame, APT steps up to the track and sets itself in the starting blocks.

There are, of course, many possible versions of APT. Here is a description of the one entered in this race:

Macroeconomic Factors:

The monthly return on Treasury bills

The difference in the monthly return on long- and short-term
    Treasury bonds

The difference in the monthly return on Treasury bonds and
    low-grade corporate bonds of the same maturity

The monthly change in the consumer price index

The monthly change in industrial production

The beginning-of-month dividend-to-price ratio for the S&P 500

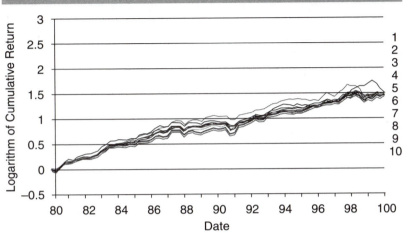

FIGURE 13–3 Logarithm of Cumulative Decile Performance, CAPM

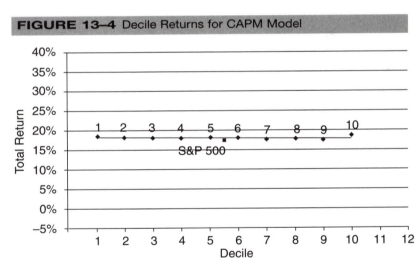

FIGURE 13–4 Decile Returns for CAPM Model

Beta Estimation:

Regress each stock's monthly return on the six macroeconomic factors over the trailing 48–60 months depending on data availability. Betas are reestimated monthly.

Payoff Estimation:

The payoff to each macroeconomic beta is projected as the mean of the trailing 12 monthly payoffs.

Some may dispute the credentials of this particular APT model. But they can enter their contestants in races that will be held in the future.

Our APT is ready. Once again, the starter fires, and the computer begins to hum.

APT runs a little longer than CAPM. Once it has crossed the finish line, we are ready to examine APT's predictive prowess. The results are exhibited in Figure 13–5.

Anemic.

At least it's not perverse. Decile 5 comes in first, but decile 10 finishes second, and decile 1 last.

But the spreads are not at all impressive.

The average annualized rates of return to the deciles are plotted in Figure 13–6. APT shows a spread of 4.68% between one end of the line-of-best-fit and the other.

In assessing these results, we should keep in mind that APT had an inherent advantage over CAPM in the race. In ranking the deciles by beta, we forced CAPM to project forward its prediction—a *positive* payoff to risk. Its dismal performance can be attributed to the fact that it was forced to run the race on a track where the true payoff to risk is actually negative.

CAPM would have done considerably better if we had estimated the monthly payoff to market beta and then projected forward the average of the trailing 12 payoffs, as we did with APT.

The judges are ready to post the final results. They can be seen in Exhibit 13–1.

It's not even close.

The New Finance takes the gold!

Let me now turn to the army of Modern Finance and say, as subtly as possible,

"We can predict **much** better than you!!!"

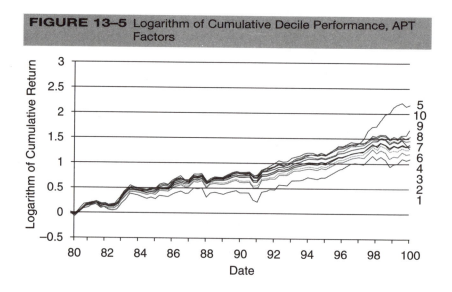

FIGURE 13–5 Logarithm of Cumulative Decile Performance, APT Factors

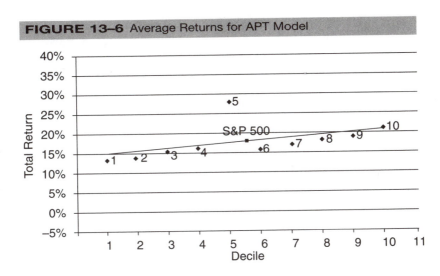

FIGURE 13–6 Average Returns for APT Model

EXHIBIT 13–1

RESULTS OF THE GREAT RACE

THE RUNNER FROM THE NEW FINANCE:

Ad Hoc Expected-Return Factor Model:
Average Annualized Spread Between Deciles 1 and 10:   38.27
Years with Negative Spreads: 0 years

THE RUNNERS FROM MODERN FINANCE:

CAPM:
Average Annualized Spread Between Deciles 1 and 10:   −.089%
Years with Negative Spreads: 13 years

APT:

Average Annualized Spread Between Deciles 1 and 10:   7.97%
Years with Negative Spreads: 6 years

AFTERTHOUGHTS

After seeing the relatively low predictive power of the models of modern finance, you might ponder their practical value in investments and corporate finance. It appears that the CAPM would tend to lead investment managers to the wrong end of the performance spectrum. The APT might tend to give you a nudge toward the right end, but given its relatively low power, your clients must be very patient in waiting for the appearance of superior returns. Unfortunately, patience does not rule in the investment business. Investment managers must face periods of narrow markets, where a few stocks account for the lion's share of the performance of the cap-weighted S&P 500 Index. They must also face periods of high volatility, where random, unpredictable factors dominate relative performance. To assure themselves of a reasonable probability of success, investment managers must follow the most powerful signals to add value to their clients' portfolios. This author is personally aware of at least one firm that attempted to manage institutional money using the APT to estimate their expected returns. After prolonged periods of disappointing performance and the loss of clients, the firm decided to add to their factor model many of the fundamental factors (such as book-to-price) discussed in this book.

Notes

1. M. Brennan, T. Chordia, and A. Subrahmanyam, "Cross-Sectional Determinants of Expected Returns," *Working Paper,* University of California, Los Angeles, April 16, 1997.

2. Similar comments were made at a conference where the paper was initially presented.

3. Because the portfolios are formed by ranking on book-to-market, they will be heterogeneous with respect to this variable. BCS actually run several tests in which they form portfolios on the basis of different variables after ranking on size. They make much of the fact that their results change greatly, depending on how the portfolios are formed. The fact that the results change doesn't surprise us, considering the portfolios are likely to be fairly homogeneous in the variables not used in portfolio formation. The likely effect of this would be to make the regression coefficients unstable from model to model.

4. Similar to factor analysis.

5. They do this by regressing the stock returns on the returns to the five portfolios over the entire period of their study.

6. See K. French and R. Roll, "Stock Return Variances: The Arrival of Information and the Reaction of Traders," *Journal of Financial Economics,* 1986. French and Roll (FR) find that on those Wednesdays in 1968 when the New York Stock Exchange closed to catch up on paperwork, the volatility of stock prices was a tiny fraction of its value when the exchange was open. During the hours of normal trading on those Wednesdays, all other sources of information relevant to the pricing of stocks were going full blast. The only source of information shut down was the changes in the prices of the stocks themselves. Rather than come to the obvious conclusion that a major component of stock volatility is driven by reactions to changes in stock prices (a conclusion that would be inconsistent with inefficient markets), FR conclude that investors simply stop looking for new information when the market is closed because they must wait until the market is open to act on it. In *Beast on Wall Street,* I refer to this as the Preposterous Private Information Hypothesis.

14

THE ROADS TO HEAVEN AND HELL

GOURMET PORTFOLIO MANAGEMENT

In Chapter 10, we discussed the general strategy employed by most value managers.

Starting from a base population of U.S. stocks, these managers first screen by size, working their way into a small-, mid- or large-cap subpopulation. Then they screen by some measure or measures of cheapness, working their way into a population of perhaps 200 stocks, all of which are cheap and all of which fit into the particular size category.

Then they attempt to "go around the corner," through a subjective evaluation of each firm's prospects. Basically, they're trying to find firms that are selling cheap in the market, but have reasonably good prospects nevertheless.

Take a look at the stocks in their portfolio, and you will find that they are uniform in at least two respects. They are all of similar size, and they are all selling cheap.

In fact, given the way most pension funds manage their equity composites, the holdings had better be uniform in nature. Pension funds hire managers as though they were pieces in a puzzle.

This piece is large-cap growth, this is small-cap value, etc.

When the pieces are assembled, they form a composite that looks pretty much like the market. And that's the way the pension officers like it. If they invest in the market, they can't be beaten by it.

But this works only if they can count on the nature of each piece of the puzzle. So a value manager had better not be found with Microsoft in the portfolio.

Think about this: Can you imagine *cooking* like institutional money managers *invest?*

First, you would think about how the final dish should taste. Then you screen the ingredients so that each tastes like you want the final dish to taste. Having screened the ingredients, you then attempt to "go around the corner" by selecting the tastiest and cooking them for the right amount of time and at the right temperature.

Good luck. And thanks, but I think I'll pass on that dinner invitation.

125

FIGURE 14–1 The Roads to Heaven and Hell

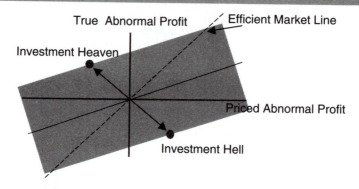

Great chefs don't cook that way.

Instead they think about the contribution that each ingredient makes to the taste of the final dish. They wouldn't even imagine requiring each ingredient to stand on its own in terms of the way that it tastes.

Most people don't care for the taste of raw eggs. Only a few of us would sit before a plateful of anchovies and lick our chops. And how often have you snacked on a few cloves of garlic?

But put these together with some lettuce and Parmesan cheese, and you've got a great Caesar salad.

Again, a great chef thinks about the *contribution* that each ingredient will make to the taste of the *final dish,* not about the taste of each ingredient on its own.

That's the way we should build stock portfolios.

You're going to eat that tasty dish all at once *as a whole,* not each ingredient *one at a time.*

In the same sense, you're going to invest in the portfolio *as a whole.* You're not going to invest in each stock individually in turn, *say, one day at a time—* IBM on the first day of the month, General Motors on the second, and so on.

Because you're investing in them all simultaneously, there's no reason to require each stock in your portfolio to look essentially like every other, in terms of its character.

As we see in Figure 14–1, you can't get to Investment Heaven by going around the corner.

Instead you must go directly to Heaven.

GOING DIRECTLY TO HEAVEN AND STRAIGHT TO HELL

In going directly to Investment Heaven, you build your portfolio as you would build a wonderful company through a merger and acquisition program. You specify the way you want your portfolio to look, and then you assemble the profile piece-by-piece by bringing together companies that make their own individual contributions to the desired character.

This is easily done as part of the portfolio optimization process.

Remember Exhibit 5–1? It laid out the constraints imposed on the optimized $L, I,$ and H portfolios. No more than 5% could be invested in one stock. The investment in any one industry was restricted to within 3% of the investment in that industry by the Russell 1000 stock index.

Investment weight restrictions aren't the only constraints we can apply to the optimization.

How about requiring that the portfolio's average return on equity be in the upper 10th percentile relative to the underlying stock population? How about requiring that the portfolio's average book-to-price ratio be in the upper 10th percentile *as well.*

Feed the optimizer fundamental information as well as expected returns and correlations. Let it build the profile you want with its linear programming abilities.

In terms of Figure 14–1, we can move, in this way, directly to Heaven and straight to Hell.

You will find that you can be very demanding in terms of the nature of the profile you require.

How demanding?

Table 14–1 shows the characteristics of two 27-stock portfolios constructed on January 19, 1998, from a population of 1,200 of the largest U.S. stocks. In building the Super Stock portfolio, we required that its average earnings-, dividend-, cash flow-, sales-, and book-to-price ratios all be in the upper 10th percentile relative to the stock population. On average, the stocks in the portfolio must be selling very cheap in the market. However, we also want the portfolio to be composed of very profitable companies. Therefore, we required that its average profit margin, return on assets, return on equity, and five-year trailing growth in earnings per share all be in the upper 10th percentile of the population.

In building the Stupid Stock portfolio, we did exactly the opposite.

The character of the Super Stock portfolio is truly magnificent. And the Stupid Stock portfolio is truly disgusting. But what did you expect from two portfolios residing respectively in Investment Heaven and Hell?

Could we even come close to these profiles using hierarchical screens? Let's try.

On January 19, 1998, 8.13% was at the upper 10th earnings-to-price percentile. This, of course, would screen all but 120 stocks from the base population.

The upper 10th percentile in terms of profit margin was 18.12%. The two screens taken together screen out all but 13 stocks.

The upper 10th percentile for dividend-to-price was 5.27%. The three screens remove all but 2 stocks.

The upper 10th percentile for trailing earnings growth was 42.77%. That screens them all out. There is no single stock in the upper 10th percentile for each of these measures of cheapness and profitability.

Table 14–1 Characteristics of Super and Stupid Stock Portfolios (Jan. 19, 1998)

Characteristics	Super	Stupid	S&P 500
Market Beta (trailing 3–5 years)	.673	.901	1.00
Market Capitalization	$20B	$13B	$56B
Earnings-to-Price	8.13%	−3.15%	4.37%
Cash Flow-to-Price	17.36	−1.31	7.48
Dividend-to-Price	5.27	.55	1.99
Sales-to-Price	353.75	21.33	64.50
Book-to-Price	74.03	14.00	27.03
Profit Margin	18.12	−42.82	10.18
Return on Assets	12.33	−7.65	7.56
Return on Equity	28.99	−9.47	21.18
Earnings Growth (trailing 3–5 years)	42.78	−10.42	15.49

But you can easily build a *portfolio* that is in the upper 10th percentile for these and many more.

Stop eating investment slop.

It's time to start dining at Joel Rubuchon's in Paris.

AFTERTHOUGHTS

The numbers of Table 14–1 are simple averages of the individual characteristics across the individual stocks in the portfolios. You might think about taking the "Super Stock" portfolio construction process one step beyond a simple averaging process. In this case, you actually assume that you buy a piece of each company in accord with the percentage allocated to each company in the portfolio and the total amount invested in each stock. Here you calculate the characteristics of your "conglomerate" portfolio on a pro-forma basis.

How might this affect your calculations of the portfolio's characteristics? Consider the calculation of combined interest coverage across the portfolio. Suppose you invest equally in two stocks of equal size, each having $1,000 in operating income. One company has $100 in interest (interest coverage of 10X); the other has $1 in interest (interest coverage of 1000X). If you combined the two companies, they would have total operating income of $2000 and $101 in interest, for an interest coverage number of 19.8X. A simple average of the coverage numbers (as per Table 14–1) would give you a figure of 505X—a clear difference. If the philosophy of the "Super Stock portfolio construction process" is taken to be one of constructing a collection of stocks such that, if they were actually merged together, the combined company would possess outstanding characteristics, then pro-forma calculations of the characteristics would seem to make sense.

Pro-forma calculations make a difference for some characteristics but not for others. You might think about which of the characteristics can and cannot be averaged.

15

THE WRONG 20-YARD LINE

―――⟨⟨⟨⟩⟩⟩―――

THE TRILOGY

As you know, this book is the third in a trilogy about the behavior of stock market prices. *The New Finance* focused on the market's major systematic mistake. In failing to appreciate the strength of competitive forces in a market economy, it over-estimates the length of the short run. In doing so, it over-reacts to records of success and failure for individual companies, driving the prices of successful firms too high and their unsuccessful counterparts too low. It is now well-documented that today's successful firms tend to experience negative earnings surprises down the road, while the unsuccessful benefit from positive surprises.[1] To try to attribute these highly significant differential reactions around earnings announcement days to differentials in risk is, quite simply, *preposterous*.

Beast on Wall Street focuses on stock volatility. It contends that stock volatility has three components. Rational and unbiased responses of stock market prices to real, economic events are the source of *event-driven volatility*. In an efficient market, this is the only component of volatility. If the market is inefficient, prices over-react to some types of information and underreact to others.[2] These misguided reactions to real, economic events create a second component of volatility called *error-driven volatility*. Expected-return factor models, like the one described in this book, largely exploit error-driven volatility. Finally, we have *price-driven volatility*—price changes that occur as reactions to previous price changes, as opposed to real, economic events. *Beast* makes a case for the fact that, in a normal market period, 80% of the variance of stock returns is price driven. This redundant component of volatility serves to dramatically increase the risk premium on equities and serves as a permanent drag on investment spending and economic growth. Price-driven volatility is also *explosive*. In October 1997, price-driven volatility in stock and currency markets exploded worldwide. On Oct. 27, 1997, the implied volatility of options on the S&P 100 Stock Index more than doubled, spiking at 50%. This occurred in reaction to the severe drop in Asian markets. These markets were reacting to their own volatility bursts; the U.S. market reacted in turn on Monday; the Asians then reacted to the United States on Tuesday. Price changes in one market are driven by price changes in another, an impressive and undeniable demonstration of price-driven volatility. In this case economic activity in Asia suffered dramatically; volatility cooled quickly in the United States however, and the U.S. economy was spared.

This book, *The Inefficient Stock Market,* focused on expected-return factor models, which, in part, attempt to exploit error-driven volatility. The positive payoff to cheapness results from the market's overreaction to success and failure. The positive payoff to intermediate-term momentum results from the market's underreaction to positive and negative surprises in individual earnings reports.

However, expected-return factor models also exploit the distortions in the structure of stock prices brought about by price-driven volatility. Price reactions to price changes undoubtedly contribute significantly to *imprecision* in stock pricing. And, as we know, imprecision drives the positive payoff to profitability.

AMATEUR NIGHT AT THE FINANCIAL CIRCUS

To more fully understand the three components of stock volatility, consider the following example. Imagine that there are a number of aerialists on a wire high above the circus floor. No net. Each holds a balance bar. Let's let the wire represent the economy, each aerialist the market for a particular stock, and movements in the balance bars represent fluctuations in the stock prices.

The wire, or the economy, is subject to a series of real economic and financial events or shocks. Each event occurs at a different point on the wire, in different proximity to each of the individual aerialists. If they want to stay on the wire, the aerialists must respond individually to the events by making appropriate adjustments in their balance bars. Think of the *best adjustments humanly possible.* These movements in the balance bars represent event-driven volatility. And if the aerialists were truly the best, that's all we would see. But experts they are not. Indeed, what we may have here is *amateur night at the financial circus.* As amateurs, the aerialists over- and under-react to the various shocks to the wire. The additional component to the movements in the balance bars represents error-driven volatility.

Again, being less-than-perfect experts, the aerialists look to their colleagues for guidance. Rather than focus their attention on the wire, they begin watching the other aerialists for signals to help adjust their own balance bars. But, at the same time, the *other* aerialists are also watching *them.* One bar moves in response to a shock to the wire. Another aerialist reacts to the movement in the bar—quite possibly this aerialist over-reacts. Then a third aerialist over-reacts, in turn, to the over-reaction of the second. This dynamic interaction between the aerialists can become excessive and unstable. *This* is price-driven volatility, and the evidence set forth in *Beast on Wall Street* indicates that it accounts for the greatest fraction of the movement in the balance bars.

Price-driven volatility makes the high-wire act much more dangerous than it needs to be. Fear of falling makes the aerialists require a high level of compensation in order to perform. In the stock market, a high level of price-driven volatility leads to a high premium in the required return to stock investing. The high cost of equity capital reduces the level of corporate investment spending over the long term, creating a significant drag on economic growth that eventually compounds to a tremendous difference.

The dynamic interactions between the balance bars can be explosive. Sudden, violent movements in the balance bars may create their own shocks to the wire. Consumers and corporate investors may take stock volatility seriously, creating increased uncertainty about future economic conditions. Uncertainty increases the value of the option to wait. Should you buy a full-size or a luxury car? Should you build a plant that produces a standard or deluxe version of the product? Increased uncertainty increases the probability of making the wrong decision *if* you move *now*. Instability in price-driven volatility may have important short-term effects on the level of economic activity.

Yes, the stock market is known to be a leading indicator of economic activity. But why? Does the stock market *anticipate* what is coming or does it actually *cause* what comes?

THE MONETARY AND FISCAL POLICY OF THE STOCK MARKET

As I write, we are in the midst of a rather prolonged period of dramatically high stock volatility. In Figure 15–1, I have plotted the *monthly* decile slopes of the model plotted in Figure 13–2. That is, Figure 13–2 shows the slope across the deciles for the full period of the Great Race, while Figure 15–1 plots the magnitude of the slopes month-to-month over the period 1980 through 2000. Note that, beginning in November of 1999, the slopes begin swinging *wildly*. Following November, the performance of the model swings back and forth from extremely good to extremely bad. While the *expected* performance of the model remains high, the standard error around this expectation suddenly explodes in November.

This explosion is coincident, and is likely caused by an explosion in the spread of cross-sectional differences in returns from stock to stock in any given month. The market's monthly cross-sectional volatility is the standard deviation of the differences between each of the roughly 3,500 individual stock returns and the monthly average return across the 3,500 stocks. During this recent period, cross-sectional volatility was higher than at any

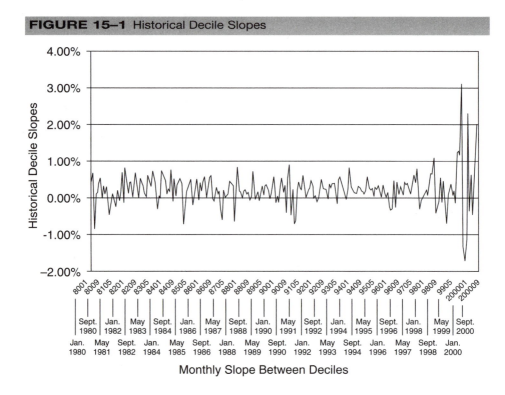

FIGURE 15–1 Historical Decile Slopes

Monthly Slope Between Deciles

other time in the history of the stock market. You must go all the way back to the middle of the Great Depression to find a period of cross-sectional volatility that even comes close.

The longitudinal (month-to-month) volatility of the return to the market averages has also been very high for a prolonged period. For example, it is no longer unusual to see an absolute daily return of 3% on the NAS-DAQ. The longitudinal volatility of the broader indexes is 70% higher than normal.

As is normally the case, the recent high level of volatility was followed by a bear market, and we now appear to be entering a period of decline in economic activity.

Many are blaming the Federal Reserve for the decline. The Fed did, after all, raise short-term interest rates by 100 basis points in 2000.

Few, however, consider that the stock market runs its own "monetary policy"

In my opinion it is the stock market's price-driven volatility that deserves nearly all of the blame for the current slump in economic activity. Under reasonable assumptions, the risk premium in the cost of equity capital is proportional to the expected *longitudinal variance* (as opposed to standard deviation or volatility) of stock returns. If volatility is up by 70%, variance is nearly three times higher than normal. This means that, for the future period over which the high volatility is expected to persist, the risk premium in the expected future return to common stock is also roughly three times its normal level. Most would consider 4% a reasonable number for the market's normal risk premium. If true, it's likely that the increase in the cost of equity induced by higher market volatility is *much* greater that the decrease in short-term interest rates induced by the Fed.

But the effect on the cost of capital is not the end of the story of the stock market's "monetary policy." Just as the Fed, intentionally or not, sends economic signals to consumers and corporate investors, so does the stock market. As discussed above, high levels of market uncertainty lead to uncertainty on the part of consumers and corporate investors about future economic conditions. This increases the value of the options to wait to consume and invest.

Thus, the stock market has an effect on economic activity analogous to, but stronger than, that of monetary policy. However, it also has an effect that is analogous to, but stronger than, *fiscal policy.* Again, as I write, politicians are talking about a tax cut that will total more than $1 trillion over the next decade. But the aggregate decline in stock prices suffered in the *last year* has been *much* larger than that.

As discussed in *Beast on Wall Street,* the recent increase in stock volatility should be expected to have a depressing effect on the *level* of stock prices. Professors of finance might argue that the stock market decline, which began in early 2000, came in anticipation of the current economic slowdown. However, few even seriously considered the possibility of an economic slump until late in the year. Surely those at the Fed didn't, because they were still raising interest rates at mid-year. Higher stock volatility increases the expected return required by stock investors to go through the financial storm. Given earnings and dividend expectations, the only path to getting the higher return *in the future* is to discount or lower the level of stock prices *now.* The decline in stock prices during 2000 is more likely a product of higher volatility than an anticipation of economic decline.

Thus, stock volatility also creates an important wealth effect[3] on those who own stock that may also depress the level of consumption. Given the fact that most of us now own stock, this final effect is now more important than ever.

Given this overall picture, blame directed at the Federal Reserve has been misplaced. The stock market has caused the slump, and, in this writer's opinion, the "monetary and fiscal policy" of the stock market is likely to be a much more important factor in influencing future economic activity than the monetary policy of the Federal Reserve or, for that matter, future tax cuts that may be enacted by Congress.

IT'S TOUGH TO BEAT THE MARKET

Were the market efficient, there would be only one component to volatility. Event-driven volatility stems from timely and unbiased reactions to economic and corporate events. If this were the only component, stock volatility would be but a small fraction of what it is today.

In *The New Finance* and *The Inefficient Stock Market,* I have laid out a "veritable *mountain* of evidence" that error-driven volatility is a significant part of the total.

And now a troublesome question:

In the presence of all these under- and over-reactions, why isn't it easy for professional investors to beat their benchmarks?

Why isn't it, in fact, like "taking candy from a baby?"

Two reasons.

First, many professional investors are victims of their own agency problems. If the market's major systematic error is overestimating the short run, the most straightforward way to exploit it is to invest in stocks earning negative abnormal profits. But these stocks won't look so good to your clients. You will have a lot of explaining to do. You see, it's not easy being a value manager. Why travel the hard road? Invest in companies that look good, instead. But given the market's major mistake, unless you're very careful about the prices you pay for these stocks, you're destined to underperform over long horizons.

Many growth stock managers aren't so careful.

Second, and more importantly, it's hard to beat the market because there is a gale of unpredictable price-driven volatility standing between you and the "candy."

Price-driven volatility creates tremendous distortions in stock prices, sending a truly overpriced stock to even greater heights and beating down an underpriced stock even more.

Price-driven volatility is the major reason why our expected-return factor model was able to explain, on average, only 10% of the differences in stock returns in a given month. Price-driven volatility is unpredictable, and it increases the element of *chance* in investment performance *dramatically.*

Proponents of the efficient market like to point to the lack of success of professionals as proof that they are correct about market efficiency. Well, we can think of a spectrum of efficiency in market pricing.

Let this spectrum take the form of an American football field: a playing field of 100 yards between two end zones. Modern Finance defends the *left* end zone. The New Finance, the *right.* On the extreme left of the playing field, we have the efficient market of Eugene Fama. In this market, there is no place for active investment because there are no under- or overvalued stocks. Wise investors invest passively. In this market, models based on rational economic behavior do a wonderful job in explaining and predicting market pricing. At this end of the field, all volatility is event-driven.

Then there is the right extreme. Here the market pays no attention whatsoever to fundamentals. *All* the volatility is price-driven. At this extreme, the market, in the short term, is in a state of complete and unpredictable chaos.

Interesting things happen as you proceed from the left side of the playing field toward the right.

Models based on rational economic behavior begin to lose power. As you pass midfield, behavioral models may begin to dominate. However, as you approach the extreme right, behavioral models may eventually lose power as well. To a great extent, these models focus on bias in behavioral reactions to real economic events. At the extreme right, the market doesn't react to real economic events. It reacts only to *its own* events. Here, the aerialists pay no attention to the wire whatsoever.

As you move from the extreme left, active investment managers gain power. However, as you cross midfield, and as unpredictable, price-driven volatility begins to dominate, the ability of active managers to outperform begins to erode.

Finally, at the right extreme, active managers will find it nearly as impossible to beat the index as they do on the left.[4] A lack of clear success by professionals simply implies that we are likely in the vicinity of *either* extreme of the efficiency spectrum.

An increasing number of academics have become critics of the efficient-market hypothesis. However, based on discussions with many of them, I feel that they believe the market is reasonably efficient. If these people were to take a position on the playing field, they would likely position themselves on the left side—say, on the 20-yard line.

Allow me to distinguish myself in this respect. I also stand on a 20-yard line, but I stand on the 20-yard line that is positioned on the *right side* of the field.

It is my feeling that price-driven volatility puts us much closer to the right than to the left. Price-driven volatility *is* unstable. When it explodes, the market's position on the field may approach the ten or even the five-yard line. When THE BEAST hibernates, as it did in 1996, the market may cross the 50-yard line into the opposite end of the field.

However, *on average,* the market resides in the vicinity of the right end zone.

THE TRIUMPH

Because *obsolescence* is once again on the line, expect the war to be long and bitter.

Most of the proponents of Modern Finance do not know the craft of investing. They aren't trained to analyze accounting statements, estimate expected returns, and effectively manage risk.

Instead, they *arrogantly* feature the mathematical *elegance* of their models. Granted, they have constructed an impressive array of mathematical paradigms, all fully consistent with the concept of rational economic behavior. Only *they* can fully appreciate how truly elegant their paradigms really are.

But good science moves back and forth between newly discovered empirical evidence and modifications of theoretical constructs that explain the evidence and make new predictions that serve to guide the future work of the empiricists.

This is how we progress toward the truth.

Isaac Newton conducted experiments with falling objects and prisms before developing his theories on gravity and light—theories that worked well in the vicinity of planet Earth and were to prevail for many years. However, in the 19th century, experiments on the speed of light produced results that contradicted Newtonian thinking.

An anomaly.

Early in the 20th century, a physicist named Albert Einstein responded by introducing his theory of relativity, which explained the anomaly and produced further predictions, many of which have since been confirmed by the empiricists.

Back and forth. This is how good science progresses toward the truth.

But Modern Finance is not good science.

The professors of Modern Finance are frustrated. They find themselves unable to go back and forth.

For good reason.

You see, they are trained to theorize *only* under the paradigm of rational economic behavior. And the evidence set forth in these books simply cannot be explained under this paradigm.

So, rather than explain, they deny. They try to nullify—or they simply choose to ignore.

What can be easily explained by moving from the rationality paradigm?

Progress blocked by the prospect of *obsolescence*.

Proponents of the New Finance stress power over elegance—*predictive power*. These proponents think the professors of Modern Finance should be far less arrogant, because their elegant models have very low *explanatory power,* and, more important, very low *predictive power*.

Elegant but *empty*.

Investors don't pay for elegance. They pay for predictive power. CEOs think elegance is irrelevant. They *pay* for predictive power. What ultimately counts is effectiveness, not the appearance of perfection.

So you see, in the end, it is nearly certain that the *power of prediction* must triumph over the *arrogance of elegance*.

Truth *will* make its way to the surface.

Notes

1. See, for example, R. La Porta, et al., "Good News for Value Stocks: Further Evidence on Market Efficiency," *Journal of Finance,* June 1997.

2. For example, the market can be said to under-react to announcements of share repurchase programs and over-react to success on the part of business firms.

3. Is the wealth effect real or partially an illusion? For those who believe in efficient markets, it is real. They believe that, given the current state of information, you can buy or sell an unlimited amount of any given stock at its current price. Thus, for them, the wealth of Bill Gates really did halve in the year 2000. If supply and demand aren't unlimited at the current price, the aggregate wealth level represented by current stock prices isn't really accessible. Therefore, Bill wasn't really as rich as some may have thought he was at the beginning of 2000.

4. Keep in mind that the source of the technical patterns we detected in stock returns result from market over- and under-reactions to real world events. At the right extreme of the spectrum, these patterns wouldn't exist. However, by buying future dividend streams at relatively cheap prices, active money managers should still be able to outperform over the long run. Over short horizons, chance will dominate relative performance.

GLOSSARY

Arbitrage Pricing Theory. Theory predicting the linear relationships between factor betas and expected stock return, enforced by arbitrageurs searching for riskless, zero-investment opportunities.

Bias. Aspect of inefficient market pricing whereby the market tends to underestimate the power of competitive entry and exit and thereby overestimates the length of the short run.

Capital asset pricing model. Theory based on the assumption of universal, unrestricted use of portfolio optimization, predicting market beta as the sole determinant of expected stock return.

Cheapness. The magnitude of a stock's current market price in relation to various measures of a stock's current level of success or profitability, such as current sales, cash flow, earnings, or dividends.

Definitional identity. A statement of the relationship between variables that owes its validity solely to the way the variables have been defined.

Diversifiable risk. Component of return variance caused by things specific to an individual firm.

Efficient market line. Line on the market map where Priced Abnormal Profit is equal to True Abnormal Profit.

Error-driven volatility. Component of stock volatility stemming from over- and under-stock price reactions to new information relevant to efficient stock pricing.

Event-driven volatility. Component of stock volatility stemming from instantaneous and unbiased stock price reactions to new information relevant to efficient stock pricing.

Expected-return factor model. Statistical model that interfaces expected payoffs with

the portfolio characteristics to obtain estimates of portfolio expected return.

Growth-stock portfolio. Portfolio containing stocks selling at relatively expensive prices as compared to accounting numbers such as sales, cash flow, earnings, and book value. Growth stocks are usually relatively profitable as well.

Imprecision. Aspect of inefficient market pricing whereby the market assigns the same price to stocks that have different potentials for abnormal profit and different prices to stocks with the same potential for abnormal profit.

Intrigue. The extent to which a company's legal/economic/political situation creates an interest in the company's stock in the media, the general public, and analysts.

Investment heaven. Place in the northwest portion of the market map where stock portfolios that are both cheap and profitable reside.

Investment hell. Place on the southeast portion of the market map where stock portfolios that are both expensive and unprofitable reside.

Normal profit. A fair profit, given the firm's risk and required capital investment.

Optimization. Mathematical procedure for finding the portfolio with the lowest possible risk, given investment constraints and an expected return objective.

Long run. Length of time over which all factors of production, including the amount of capital invested in a line of business, are subject to change.

Priced abnormal profit. The risk-adjusted present value of a firm's future abnormal profits that are reflected in the firm's current stock price.

Price-driven volatility. Component of stock volatility stemming from stock price reactions to previous changes in stock prices.

Risk-factor model. Statistical model that interfaces portfolio factor betas with factor correlations to obtain estimates of portfolio risk.

Short run. Time period over which many of the firm's means of production can't be changed, including the amount of capital investment in the line of business.

Stylized benchmark. Stock index, usually weighted by total market capitalization, that has the characteristics of a particular investment management style such as value or growth.

Technical payoff. Component of return that can be statistically related to some aspect of the previous history of a stock's performance.

True abnormal profit. The best possible estimate of the risk-adjusted present value of a firm's future abnormal profits.

Stupid stock portfolio. A portfolio containing stocks that are, on average, highly risky, illiquid, in financial distress, unprofitable, yet selling at a high price in the market.

Super stock portfolio. A portfolio containing stocks that are, on average, low risk, liquid, financially sound, highly profitable, yet selling cheaply in the market.

Systematic risk. Component of return variance attributable to the responsiveness of stock returns to factors like inflation and industrial production.

Value stock portfolio. Portfolio containing stocks selling at relatively cheap prices as compared to accounting numbers such as sales, cash flow, earnings, and book value. Value stocks are usually relatively unprofitable as well.